if he's not the one, who is?

if he's not the one, who is?

WHAT WENT WRONG— AND WHAT IT TAKES TO *find mr. right*

lisa steadman

Author of *It's a Breakup, Not a Breakdown*

POLKA DOT
press

Avon, Massachusetts

The Polka Dot Press® name and logo design
are registered trademarks of F+W Media, Inc.

Published by Polka Dot Press,
an imprint of Adams Media, a division of F+W Media, Inc.
57 Littlefield Street, Avon, MA 02322. U.S.A.
www.adamsmedia.com

ISBN 10: 1-60550-358-4
ISBN 13: 978-1-60550-358-5

Printed in the United States of America.

10 9 8 7 6 5 4 3 2 1

Library of Congress Cataloging-in-Publication Data
is available from the publisher.

This publication is designed to provide accurate and authoritative information
with regard to the subject matter covered. It is sold with the understanding that
the publisher is not engaged in rendering legal, accounting, or other professional advice. If legal advice or other expert assistance is required, the services
of a competent professional person should be sought.
—From a *Declaration of Principles* jointly adopted by a Committee of the
American Bar Association and a Committee of Publishers and Associations

Many of the designations used by manufacturers and sellers to distinguish their
product are claimed as trademarks. Where those designations appear in this
book and Adams Media was aware of a trademark claim, the designations have
been printed with initial capital letters.

This book is available at quantity discounts for bulk purchases.
For information, please call 1-800-289-0963.

To all the single women of the world who are ready to walk away from dating and relationship drama, disappointment, and disasters, and instead re-create their happily ever after. . . .

Today is your day.
To your success!
xoxo,
Lisa

acknowledgments

This book would not have happened without the love, support, and dedication of so many people. Many thanks to my fabulous editor Chelsea King, my amazing agent Sharlene Martin, my phenomenal coach Gina Ratliffe, my A+ assistant Laura Manning, and the many incredible women I work with in my coaching practice. Thank you all for making this book possible and meaningful!

And to the people in my life who support me personally . . . my parents, my sister Staci, my *amazing* friends. Thanks for being part of my Woohoo Crew! And, of course, to my very best friend in the world, my husband Luis. From the moment we met, you got what I was about, who I really am, and where I wanted to go in life. Together, this journey has been exciting, adventurous, and always full of surprises. I love, admire, and adore you!

contents

contents

preface

I'm single. Again. I'm 32 and single again.

There, I'd confessed my darkest sins.

Wait. *I'm 32 and single again and I feel like a total failure at love.*

That was the tough love truth. And it stung. The year was 2003. And while my best friends were all settled or settling down with their annoyingly adorable husbands, I was nowhere near the road to happily ever after.

Was that even what I wanted anymore? Truthfully, I didn't know. What I did know was that while I was no longer in survival mode from my Big Breakup with Mr. Ex—a journey I later chronicled online and in my first book *It's a Breakup, Not a Breakdown*—I wasn't exactly sure where this new destination was. Mr. Wrong was gone. So was the soul-crushing agony of getting over him. Somewhere between our last booty call and deleting his number from my cell phone, I was single again.

Did I feel footloose and fancy-free? Sure. But with that newfound freedom came some harsh realities. Without my breakup pain to keep me company, I felt a little lost. Empty. Alone. I actually *missed* missing my ex.

And that's not all.

If I was completely honest with myself, I was starting to feel like a failure at love. After all, the Big Breakup wasn't my first breakup. It was but one of many disastrous relationships throughout my twenties and early thirties that seemed like my very own reality show aptly titled *Loser at Love . . . Again!* And, as if on cue, at thirty-two I was starting over. Yet again.

I was living alone. Again.

I was minus a Plus One at parties. Again.

I was faced with the disappointment that Mr. Wrong was not The One. Again.

That's when the big fat fabulous truth smacked me upside my single and fabulous head.

I was free to reinvent myself. That's when the fun *really* began.

When I gave myself permission to let go of any stigma I felt about being the token single girl at parties. . . .

When I embraced the idea that my happily ever after journey might not involve a ring, a ceremony and reception, and/or the pitter patter of little feet (other than my two cats). . . .

When I woke up to the beautiful truth that because I was single I could be selfishly indulgent, quit my job, change careers, and ultimately pursue the life I'd always dreamed of, I realized that not only was I thirty-two and single—again—but I was also ready to rock my fabulous single life, BIG TIME.

I, Lisa Steadman, would date lots of wildly exciting and different men (and I did).

I, Lisa Steadman, would live my life according to my own ever-evolving rule book (sometimes casting aside the rules altogether).

I, Lisa Steadman, would take risks, ask for what I wanted, and trust that the universe would take care of me (99 percent of the time, it did).

And . . .

I, Lisa Steadman, would never, ever put myself in the position of crying over the wrong guy again (and I didn't).

Eventually, I *did* meet an exceptionally exciting and annoyingly adorable man. And while my happily-ever-after journey evolved to include a sassy strut down the aisle, I did it on my own terms.

I provided my own engagement and wedding rings (family heirlooms that I cherished).

I kept my name (if it ain't broke, why fix it?).

And the bride wore red (I looked FABULOUS!).

As for the pitter-patter of little feet, well, that hasn't changed. In our household, our two cats still hold court, but who knows?

What I *do* know is that if you're somewhere between the pain of the past and your happily-ever-after future, this book is for you. No matter how old you are, if you're single—again or for the very first time—this book is for you. Together, we'll move away from the bittersweet truth that Mr. Wrong was not The One, and into your magnificent future. A future that not only includes Mr. Next but also guides you on a journey toward your very own version of happily ever after, whatever that means for you.

Maybe you'll decide to be single and fabulous forever.

Maybe you, too, will date wildly exciting and different men until you find your perfect partner (AKA Mr. Right).

Maybe one day you'll strut your sassy stuff down the aisle, say "I do," and enjoy the pitter patter of little feet.

Regardless of the end destination, together we're going to rock your new single and fabulous journey. First, we're going to break free of whatever's holding you back (or whatever you're holding onto from your past). Then, we'll wake up to what's possible now that Mr. Wrong is gone. From reinventing your savvy single life, to letting go of old patterns and behaviors that may be sabotaging your relationship success, to understanding the boys to avoid on the dating scene, you're going to master the art of not only waking up to your new and improved life, but also moving on to your revised happily-ever-after destination. Along the way, you're going to meet a variety of interesting and available Mr. Nexts, but you're not going to foolishly give your heart away to just anyone. Instead, you're going to apply your valuable lessons learned and, in time, manifest Mr. Right. Then and only then will you hand over the keys to your healed heart and say, "Yes!" to the fantastic future that awaits.

This book is not so much a quest to answer *Who's next?* (although you may discover that along the way). More important, this is an exciting and life-shifting journey toward the revelation of *What's next?*

If you're up to the challenge, I'm excited to be your guide. Let's get started!

before you get started . . .

Before we embark on this journey together, I want to make sure we're on the same page about one very important thing. As you take steps toward your new and improved happily ever after, you will meet and date a variety of interesting, intelligent, and available men. Your job is to simply sit back, get to know them, and decide if you'd like to see them again. (It really is that simple!) To make your job even easier, let's define the types of men you'll meet:

Mr. Next: Any guy you date who has potential. You can date Mr. Next as long as you want *until* you realize that he's not a suitable match for you and your long-term relationship goals. At that time, it's up to you to call it quits, cutting down on wasted time in the dating trenches (for both of you). To make your job easier, it's important to avoid being blinded by his "potential" and/or the physical chemistry you feel for him. Instead, keep your vision 20/20. Stay true to your ultimate goal, whatever it may be. If it's to manifest Mr. Right, then you owe it to your future to avoid being sidetracked by Mr. Next.

Mr. Right: An elusive but oh-so-worth-the-wait guy who could be your perfect partner. Far from Mr. Perfect, Prince Charming, or The One, what makes this man right for you is that you share common values and long-term relationship goals, and are equally interested in and available for commitment with one another.

P.S. You will most likely meet and date a lot of Mr. Nexts before discovering Mr. Right. That's part of the fun of your new journey. Along the way, you get to practice flirting, dating, and having fun with a variety of men until the right one for you comes along. Woohoo!

Want Additional Support?

I've created a fun—FREE—playbook and three-part audio series just for you.

Go to IfHesNotTheOneWhoIs.com/bonus to download these bonus resources now!

chapter 1

mr. wrong was not the one (and that's a good thing!)

Ding dong, Mr. Wrong is gone!

And here you are, single, fabulous, and ready to rock the rest of your amazing life. Now that the breakup's behind you, the clarity's probably setting in. Not only was Mr. Ex NOT The One, but as time goes on you're probably starting to see just how wrong he was for you. When you were with him, maybe you didn't feel free to be your most authentic self. Or maybe tending to all his wants, needs, and drama kept you from pursuing your own passions. Or maybe you'd simply outgrown him but weren't sure how to let go until recently.

Of course, just because you know in your heart of hearts that your ex wasn't the right one for you doesn't mean you're feeling totally footloose and fancy free right now. In fact, as crazy as it sounds, you may actually miss *missing* your ex. Whereas the pain, disappointment, and loss you cozied up to during your breakup recovery wasn't exactly fun, it was comfortable and familiar. Without it, where are you? That's the thing nobody really talks about—what happens *after* breakup recovery and *before* you fully experience your amazing future. It's like a big fat gray area, AKA being single again.

If you're feeling aimless, don't worry. Consider this book (and me) your trusty GPS. Together, we'll walk step-by-step, turn-by-turn, away from the pain of the past and into your brilliant and beautiful future. To kick things off, this chapter's all about the fab and fun things you have to look forward to now that you're free to live that authentic life you've been dreaming of. But first, we have some business to attend to. Specifically, it's time to face and release any stigmas, fears, and/ or stresses you currently carry as a result of looking over your shoulder at the smoldering remains of your last relationship, or staring smack dab into your single and uncertain future.

Destination Unknown

In the introduction to this book, I told you that your amazing future still exists. And it does. But after the end of your last relationship, you may be wondering what exactly your future has in store for you. Maybe the life plan you'd been working toward (married by thirty, baby by thirty-two, nesting in that dreamy home with your growing family, and so on) recently got blown to smithereens. Maybe you feel so off-course right now that you're pretty sure you're no longer on the same map. There are countless scenarios that could leave you feeling like this: Perhaps you're temporarily homeless after living with your ex for years (thank God for best friends with guest rooms!); swallowing your pride despite the fact that your ex has already moved on to his next relationship while you still spend the occasional Saturday night crying over him; or waking up, rolling over, and realizing that sleeping alone is still a very new and unusual experience for you. Regardless of where you are on the spectrum of *where you were* versus *where you're going*, we're going to get there together.

Facebook Friends Weigh In

When I asked the question *What was the hardest part about being single again following your breakup or divorce?* on Facebook, here's what some of my fab friends said. . . .

"Figuring out how to coexist while sharing friends and having the same career." —ROTEM

"Wondering how long it'll be until the next significant other." —RAMONA

"After one break-up, it was keeping my dates straight. After my subsequent relationship ended? Dealing with the loss of *his* friends and living in the same town." —JENNIFER

"Not having that significant other to lean on during the tough days. Going to events alone, especially weddings when most people are paired off." —AMY

"Having someone call me before I left work to see when I was coming home and what I wanted for dinner. Yes, he would cook for me! That was hard to part with." —L. J. MAGGIE

While you may feel a little like an alien in your new surroundings, don't worry. You're not alone. There are millions of women just like you who thought their life was going in one direction and instead they woke up one day to the realization that everything had been turned upside down. Life as it used to be no longer existed for them. From breakups and affairs, to divorces and custody battles, to standing on their own two feet in No Man's land for the first time ever (or for the umpteenth time), their questions may be your questions. . . .

How did I get here?

Who am I?

What do I do now?

Guess what? Like those other amazing women who've walked in these unsteady but fabulous shoes before you, you will survive. More than that—you're going to thrive! You just need to practice a little reinvention. For inspiration, I'll be sharing some amazing stories of reinvention throughout the book. Out of the smoldering ashes of a life that no longer worked for them, incredible women just like you have picked themselves up, dusted themselves off, and found a better future awaiting them. You will, too.

First things first. Before your rockin' reinvention can begin, let's deal with what you may still be holding onto from your past. What follows are some of the most common traps that keep women firmly obsessed with the past instead of getting excited about their amazing futures. See which traps resonate most with you.

from the *fearless female files* . . .

"The hardest part is grieving the illusion. *What might have been.* The *It's not supposed to be this way* feeling is sometimes overwhelming. I can live alone quite well, have done it in the past, and enjoy my own company. But I miss the 'good days' of the relationship and what *might have been*."—marge

Trap #1: You're Stuck in *What Could Have Been*

Do thoughts of "What could have been" keep you up at night? Are you haunted by the disappointment you feel at what your future could have looked like though it never quite materialized? If you're nodding your head right about now, I get it. I've been there, and so have so many others just like you. As women, we're genetically and socially wired to want certain things. A home, someone to love, possibly a family. When a relationship ends, it's like a part of our soul dies. The disappointment in ourselves and our inability to make love work can stifle any hopes of moving into our amazing future.

But guess what? It's time to turn down the volume on that pain and disappointment. It's time to accept that—for whatever reason—things didn't work. You did your very best. In fact, you did more than your share to ensure relationship success. You don't have to know why the relationship ended in order to move on. But you do have to give yourself permission to stop looking over your shoulder, stop obsessing about "What could've been," and instead reacquaint yourself with your present circumstances, freeing yourself up to walk step by step into that magnificent future. (For now, just keep reading.)

─────── *Famous Female Reinventors* ───────

Take a look at just some of the amazing women who were forced to reinvent themselves after life threw them a core-shaking curveball or two:

Halle Berry

After two failed marriages, this leading lady blazed her own trail, nabbing a Best Actress Oscar (a first for an African-American woman!), becoming a mother to adorable daughter

Nahla, and redefining what love means to her: "I never want to be married again. . . . I no longer feel the need to be someone's wife. I don't feel like I need to be validated by being in a marriage." From where we sit, it looks like Halle's perfecting her own winning role—as herself!

Arianna Huffington

After a public and painful divorce from her politically conservative husband, Arianna changed her politics, created *The Huffington Post*, and inspires women around the world with her courage, convictions, and class: "Fearlessness is like a muscle. I know from my own life that the more I exercise it the more natural it becomes to not let my fears run me." Amen to that, sister!

Ellen DeGeneres

In the 1990s, Ellen enjoyed enormous popularity on her hit sitcom. After announcing she was gay, her sitcom got cancelled, she retreated into oblivion, and that could have been the rest of the story. A decade later, she's back on top with her hit daytime talk show, endorsement deals, and skyrocketing popularity. A true testament to the power of perseverance, believing in yourself, and dancing to your own beat!

Elizabeth Gilbert

Reeling from a soul-crushing divorce, Elizabeth traded life in New York City for a year of solo travel, spending equal time eating in Italy, praying in an ashram in India, and learning to love again in Bali. She chronicled her adventures in *Eat, Pray, Love*, an exquisite, excruciating, and inspiring tale of recovery and renewal.

Trap #2: You Feel Like a Failure at Love

When you look back at past relationships and see that the only two common denominators are you and the fact that the relationship ended, it's easy to fall into the false assumption that you must be a failure at love. And while it's true that you participated in each and every one of those past relationships, it's also true that there was something about each of those relationships that worked for you at the time (and eventually stopped working for you). On some level (emotionally, spiritually, sexually, and so on), you got something out of it. And you stayed because that need was being fulfilled.

from the *fearless female files* . . .

"The hardest part about being single again was realizing that I'd been single all along. I was in a one-sided relationship where the other person got all their needs met while I got none of mine met. It was draining, frustrating, and depressing."—tamika

In hindsight, it's easy to look back and wonder why you stayed so long. It's also easy to start blaming yourself for wasting time and making poor choices. If you're feeling like a failure at love right about now, stop. Let's tweak your thinking.

First, is it safe to assume that every man and woman around you (friends, family members, coworkers, virtual strangers) above the age of thirty has been in at least a couple (or a handful) of relationships over the course of their lives?

If that's true—and it is—doesn't that mean that, with the exception of the current relationship they're in (if they're in one), that all of those past relationships ended?

The only logical answer is yes.

Therefore, wouldn't you say that all of those people aren't so much failures at love as they are students in the game of love, learning lessons, getting better, and playing smarter as they go along? Most of us don't "get it right" the first time, and 99 percent of us don't settle down, marry, and spend the rest of our lives with the very first person we date. In fact, by dating a variety of people, getting into and out of several relationships, we actually discover more about who we are and who could be right for us.

from the *fearless female files* . . .

"I dated this man off and on for seventeen years. We lived 70 miles apart for seventeen years. I dated him and desperately wanted to marry him and create a home with him. It was a little like chasing a dream I never could quite catch. There was always a reason or something going on, an excuse why we couldn't marry and merge households. I broke up with him for good a few months ago and have made the choice daily not to go back. I can't help feeling like I wasted too much time on him, and now I'm paying for it."—jean

Are you starting to see how the only realistic option when it comes to dating and relationships is to embrace the idea that it really is a numbers game and so, in order to succeed, you've got to play the numbers, AKA date around before settling down?

The answer is simply yes.

Let's be clear. You are not a failure at love. You, my fabulous friend, are on a journey, and your only assignment is to pay attention, learn your lessons, and apply them accordingly in your future. Moving forward, if you correctly apply whatever lessons you've learned or are learning from your last relationship, you'll never again repeat those same issues, patterns, and mistakes. In fact, if you apply the Goldilocks principle to your next relationship, learning from what did and didn't work in the past, you may even get it "just right" next time!

Trap #3: You Feel Like You Wasted Time in the Relationship

When you look in the rearview mirror of your last relationship, do you:

A. Kick yourself for staying too long?
B. Feel like you wasted weeks, months, or years of your life that you'll never get back?
C. Worry that your ex still has time to get everything he wants, but it's too late for you?
D. All of the above.

Whether you chose A, B, C, or D, the good news is that it's never too late to be true to yourself. Did you stay longer than you should have in the wrong relationship? Maybe. But you probably still had lessons to learn. Can you recoup those so-called wasted weeks, months, years? Not literally, no; but cosmically, yes. How? By learning your lessons, promising to never again repeat patterns and habits that no longer work for you, and by remaining consistently committed to your amazing future. If you commit to your successful future, you will never again waste time on the wrong guy.

As for your ex and what's now in store for him, you don't have any control over that. And that's the good news. Truthfully, it doesn't matter what happens to your ex from here on out. What matters is your fabulous self. Focusing on *your* future—that is, what you want, and how you're going to go about manifesting it—is the surest way to achieve success. That's what this book is all about.

from the *fearless female files* . . .

"The hardest part about moving on was redefining who I was and living for myself again instead of for someone else." —lisa

Trap #4: You Feel Lost

Raise your hand if you spent most of your last relationship catering to your ex's every need. There's nothing to be ashamed of. It simply means you've got a lot of love to give. Moving forward, why not put all of that amazing love and attention into your own interests, your own needs, your own self-nurturing? That way, you'll never again get lost in a relationship, living solely for the purpose of helping your partner get everything they want and need, all the while feeling suffocated, isolated, and/or underappreciated. Truthfully, in a healthy and happy relationship, wants and needs are a two-way street. You take care of yourself *and* your partner, and vice versa. Love that! In the meantime, focus all that love and attention on Y-O-U.

Trap #5: You're Scared to Be Single

When it comes to being single, what scares you the most? Standing on your own two feet? Not having a date on Saturday night? Never dating again? Never meeting your perfect partner, falling in love, and experiencing your very own version of happily ever after? All of the above?

For me, my greatest fear about being single was the fear that I would never meet somebody who could love, adore, and understand me, quirks and all. That maybe I was too independent, unconventional, and inappropriate to find love. That maybe love was for simpler, cuter, more successful, less complicated people.

Sound familiar?

The truth is, you *are* worthy of love, warts and all. Your happily ever after still exists. It's just up to you to redefine it.

In the meantime, it's okay to be scared to be single. It may be new and unfamiliar territory, but as uncomfortable as it can sometimes feel, being single is also a gift and a blessing. In time you may just discover that you actually enjoy being single. That's one of my goals in writing this book—to help you experience the exquisite pleasure of your own company, the amazing freedom in coming and going as you please, and the absolute delight in meeting someone new who gets how wonderful you really are. Whether you want to be single and fabulous forever, or hope to quickly find your perfect partner, settle down, and share your life with someone, my hope is that along the way you'll learn to enjoy the simple and joyous pleasures of being single. Of course, there are also plenty of pitfalls to being single, especially if you're the only one in your social circle who's single. Most especially if it's been years (or even decades) since anyone else you know has had to start over again.

Suddenly Single

If you're the only single person in your social circle, let me remind you that it doesn't make you a failure at love. It's important for you to really understand and embrace that, regardless of where your friends are on their happily-ever-after journeys. Life is not a competition to some end destination. Your journey is uniquely yours, heartbreak and all. Give yourself some credit for living your life as authentically as possible. The fact that your last relationship ended means that it wasn't right for you. Now's the time to celebrate your honesty, bravery, and commitment to yourself. By being willing to start over, you get to re-create your version of happily ever after. That's a beautiful thing!

from the *fearless female files* . . .

"The secret to loving your single life is to have fun and happy single friends. Girls you can just call up out of the blue and say, 'I'm in the neighborhood. Let's grab coffee, a cocktail, a cutie!' You've got to have your girls who make life interesting." —cindy

Having said that, being single can also be a frustrating experience when you're the only single person in your social circle, but don't despair. You just need to retrain your friends on how to handle your suddenly single status. Now would be an excellent time to remind them that:

1. You don't have automatic weekend plans anymore and it would be nice if they invited you over on Saturday night.
2. Yes, you're still entitled to cry over your ex even if technically you're over him.
3. Group conversations cannot be limited to engagement talk, planning a romantic vacation, and anniversary party planning, and must include at least one of the following topics: dating, workplace gossip, bikini waxing, Facebook, or *Dancing with the Stars*.
4. They need to call you at least once a week just to say hi, ask how things are going, and only mention their significant other if you ask.
5. As your friend, they need to respect your healed heart, and avoid talking about your ex unless you bring him up first (even if technically you're over him).

Single, Party of Fun

While you don't have to ditch your happily hooked-up friends, you need to start expanding your social circle to include your fellow single and fabulous friends. Don't have any? Not to worry. Here are some great ways to make like-minded friends.

1. Volunteer for a worthy cause you care about.
2. Join a singles support group. (Yes, they exist and no, you're not pathetic.)
3. Participate in community events in your neighborhood.
4. Join a networking group. (Why not grow your business while meeting new people?)
5. Take a class you'd enjoy. (Learn a new language, improve your cooking skills with a new cuisine, sharpen your artistic abilities with a painting or drawing class, and so on.)

Are you starting to see how the key to loving your life as a savvy single lies in your ability to embrace your new reality, surround yourself with supportive friends, and celebrate lessons learned? All it takes is a slight tweak to your attitude and *voila!* You're living and loving your new life.

1. Review the traps discussed in the chapter. Which, if any, resonate most as potential traps you find yourself stuck in?

2. What do you need to do to get un-stuck?

3. Make an action plan for getting un-stuck. Take steps every day to free yourself and embrace a new savvy single attitude.

Want to Share Your Results with Me?

Join my Facebook fan page. Drop me a note to tell me how you're enjoying the book so far. I'd love to hear from you!

the best mistake you'll ever make

Now that you know all the reasons you *might* be looking over your shoulder at the past, it's time to adjust your gaze and get excited about your immediate and eventual future. While you and your ex had some good times together, think of all the even better times ahead—experiences you would have missed out on completely had you stayed in the wrong relationship. In case you need reminding, here are just a few of the amazing life experiences you would have sadly skipped had you and Mr. Wrong kept going strong.

The Chance to Be Single and Fabulous

Whether you know it or not, being single is an essential step in your journey to happily ever after. It's a time in life when you get to be self-indulgent, cater to your ever-evolving personal needs, and really get to know your most authentic self. By embracing and celebrating what makes you unique you discover your purpose on the planet. In the wrong relationship, you'd never get to those truths. You'd be too busy/distracted/

17

drained from catering to Mr. Wrong's wants, needs, desires, and/or demands, all the while ignoring your gut instinct to run for the hills because the relationship never allowed you to be true to yourself. So while there may be times ahead when being a savvy single can feel like a life sentence, relish the freedom you've got right now. Celebrate the strength it took to heal and move on from Mr. Wrong. And, above all else, embrace your resilience and the lessons you're learning on a daily basis.

from the *fearless female files* . . .

"Suddenly, I was free to socialize and therefore position myself to take advantage of new opportunities in my career and personal life. I never had to second guess my instincts or take someone else's feelings into consideration before doing something that made me feel good. I had the chance to travel more, volunteer my time, get active once again in grassroots politics, and make new friends. I suddenly had a life without limit."—nikki

The Endless Possibilities of Dating

You may or may not be ready to date yet. But when you decide to get back out there (and trust me, you will!), you're going to discover the unlimited possibilities. Without ending things with your ex, you'd never realize just how many incredible, interesting, and amazing men are out there in the world. Sure, you probably have to sift through some slime balls, players, and otherwise emotionally stunted losers while you're in the dating trenches.

But hey, those make for great stories to laugh at and share with your girlfriends. Plus, when you're a truly successful single, the wrong guys quickly and easily fall by the wayside (along with any dating disappointments and other disasters) so that you're readily available to meet Mr. Next (and eventually Mr. Right).

from the *fearless female files* . . .

"When I finally had the courage to leave the relationship, my life blossomed quickly and beautifully into many, many blessings. I'm stronger, wiser, and much better. I realize I possess all the love I thought I required. And I've met so many men who find me not just attractive, but hot! It's done wonders for my ego and self-esteem. Yes, I have an ego!"—tamika

You know what else? Without the breakup, you'd never discover the joy that comes from an amazing date with someone new. You'd never experience the butterflies of first kisses with certain cuties in your future. If you'd stayed with Mr. Wrong, your next dating adventure wouldn't be just around the corner (trust me, it is!). What a shame it would be to have settled for so much less than you deserve. *Woohoo!* to you for breaking free from that so-so relationship (even if it broke free from you), healing, and moving in the direction of your fab future.

The Opportunity to Live Alone

If before the breakup you'd never lived alone, or if it had been some time since you'd shacked up by yourself, you now have the absolute pleasure of your own company on a daily basis. While it can sometimes feel lonely, scary, and/or isolating, living alone can also feel peaceful, exciting, and fun. Not only do you fully realize your own resilience by living alone, but you discover—or reclaim—your truest self. From the way you decorate your home to the dishes you eat on to the new rituals you create moving forward, being your own roommate can help make your future that much brighter.

from the *fearless female files* . . .

"You'll find that there is a comfort in solitude. Solitude leads to self-awareness and that awareness leads to empowerment. The only person you really have to go looking for is you. That's when true love will find you. Love for experience. Love for living. Love for the world around you and, yes, even romantic love." —nikki

Here are just some of the many ways you can celebrate shacking up solo:

1. Dance around your living room in your undies, singing your heart out to your fave female anthems any time of the day or night.
2. Leave dishes in the sink for an entire week without having to hear anyone complain.
3. Embrace your complete control of the TV remote.
4. Burn incense, light candles, and spray perfume without anyone complaining about their allergies.

5. Sleep naked, watch TV naked, cook naked (watch out for hot splatter!), pay bills naked, surf the Web naked . . . you get the picture.

Facebook Friends Weigh In

When I asked the question, "What do you appreciate most about having dated around rather than settled down with the first person who came along?" on Facebook, here's what some of my friends said. . . .

"You realize what you prefer and what kind of person you like being around." —DANIELLE

"Experience both good and bad. A better sense of what you like and don't like, and what you want and don't want, both in yourself and others." —LUISA

"The chance to get to know yourself, for better or worse, in between relationships." —NANCY

The Chance to Meet Someone Better Suited for You

As a savvy single, not only do you get to enjoy the endless possibilities of dating, but eventually, you get to experience the absolute pleasure of meeting someone who is so much better suited for you than your ex ever was. And whether he's Mr. Next or Mr. Right, he will most likely have some of the fantastic qualities your ex possessed (that you still miss), as well as traits that Mr. Wrong was incapable of embodying. Things you really need in a man but that your ex could never offer. Maybe it's a deeper emotional or spiritual connection. Or, someone whose vision of the future perfectly matches your own. Or maybe it's as simple as Mr. Next is a better communicator (or he makes you laugh—love that!). That's the beauty of the endless possibilities now available to you. When you meet someone who's better suited for you, you know it. You feel it. And it absolutely rocks your world.

A Renewed Sense of Peace

When you give yourself permission to let go of your past, your journey forward becomes clearer. It's like a spotlight starts shining on the path beneath your feet. A new direction takes shape. New opportunities emerge. And best of all, an inner calm and peace envelop you. By freeing yourself from what no longer works, you give yourself permission to live with passion and purpose. Truthfully, that may be the best gift of all!

Here's how a renewed sense of peace may find its way into your life:

1. You develop an interest in yoga or meditation, inviting a deeper connection to your spirituality.
2. A mentor appears, guiding you in a new and unexpected direction.
3. You take up a new hobby or enroll in a class that brings excitement and passion back into your life.
4. You decide to take on a challenge (run a marathon, save for a house, and so forth).
5. Day by day, you realize it's getting easier to forgive yourself.

Other Opportunities

Truthfully, the opportunities you would have missed out on had you stayed with your ex may not yet have revealed themselves to you. But you'll be able to recognize them as they unfold. From an unexpected career opportunity that takes you in a new and exciting direction to rewarding new friendships that materialize from people your ex never could have appreciated to fun single-gal adventures like traveling abroad, late nights with girlfriends, and saucy makeout sessions with new cuties, the opportunities are limitless. All you have to do is be open to them. And now that your ex is out of the picture, there's nothing standing between you and your fab future. So sit back, relax, and get ready to receive unexpected gifts, life lessons, and opportunities—all because you were brave enough and bold enough to believe in yourself!

from the *fearless female files* . . .

"First, nurture yourself and allow yourself to grieve. That's important. Then focus on what you can do for yourself, all the good things that didn't happen, that you didn't enjoy because 'he didn't want to,' and then start doing them!" —marge

Rewrite "Happily Never After"

Are you starting to see the many blessings that accompanied Mr. Ex's exit? Have you fully celebrated why it's good he's long gone? I hope so. If not, take time today (even right this very minute) to celebrate that fact. Better yet, do a little happy dance right now.

Your next order of business is to rewrite your happily never after, creating a more realistic relationship ending, thanks to the benefit of 20/20 hindsight. See, up until now, your breakup story has probably gone something like this:

A. He left me.
B. I left him.
A. He was an asshole.
B. I was a fool, idiot, moron.
A. I hope I never see his pathetic face again.
B. He said he never wants to see or hear from me again.
A. I'll never forgive him for the things he said/did.
B. He'll never forgive me for the things I said/did.

Sound familiar? The truth is, as you enter Successful Single-dom, it's important to loosen your grip on your Story of Us. It's time to create a new Story of You, applying lessons from your revised Story of Us as you see fit.

Let me explain. After a while, your Story of Us, gut-wrenching breakup included, can take on a life of its own. And the legend surrounding your relationship (i.e., *He was a heartless jerk, I am nothing but a massive relationship failure*) only grows larger, uglier, nastier, and so on. The danger in this scenario is that you run the risk of missing out on valuable lessons and possibly buy into limiting beliefs about what you deserve in life and love. Before you can successfully move into your amazing future, you owe it to yourself to take a more honest look at your relationship past, and how it affects the new Story of You.

Here's how: If your ex is nothing but a cheating/lying/deceitful scumbag, then he's the villain of your story. Guess that makes you the fool, victim, or loser—but that's just not true. So before you write yourself off as a complete romantic failure, or look at your entire relationship with your ex as one giant catastrophe, stop. It's time for that major happily-never-after rewrite.

In your revised story, what wonderful, amazing, valuable lessons did you learn from loving your ex? How did his presence in your life make you a better woman? How will your future be better because he was a part of your past? Without putting Mr. Wrong on a pedestal or tossing your tarnished self into the trash for having stayed too long or put up with too much, what beautiful truths can you take away from your time together?

Maybe you got clearer about the kind of partner you really want and deserve. Thanks to Mr. Ex's good qualities, as well as qualities he lacked, you may now have a sharper vision of what kind of guy would be an ideal match for you. For example:

- If your ex was a workaholic, you're now looking for someone who enjoys his job but isn't married to it.
- If among your ex's great qualities, he had an amazing sense of humor, you may choose to find a future partner who also has a sense of humor, but has other important qualities your ex lacked.
- If your ex had a tumultuous relationship with his immediate family members and you're super close to your own family, you now know the importance of finding a man who has healthy relationships with his relatives.
- If you appreciated your ex's chivalrous nature but didn't enjoy his chauvinistic qualities, you may want to be on the

lookout for a true gentleman who's got a more progressive view of gender roles.

- If your ex mismanaged his finances or was up to his eyeballs in debt (regardless of how much he made), you may now realize that it's more important to find a partner who lives well within his means than one who makes a lot of money.

In addition to getting a better idea of the kind of guy who could be right for you eventually, are you also beginning to realize that, thanks to life with your ex, you became a better woman? If so, fantastic! Silently thank Mr. Wrong for having had a positive effect on your future. If you're not sure how your ex affected you in ways other than the bitter variety, you may need to review your relationship with an objective eye or ask a friend for their input. Chances are your ex contributed at least a handful of valuable life lessons. The following are just a few examples of how your ex may have helped shape you into a more amazing woman:

- Because he was health conscious, you discovered your love for healthy eating and exercise and now look and feel fantastic.
- Thanks to your ex's fiscal fitness, you now have a solid financial plan for the future.
- With your ex's encouragement, you went back to school, pursued a better job, and/or made a necessary life change that's rocking your fantastic future.
- Even though he wasn't right for you, the love and encouragement Mr. Ex gave you have made you a more confident individual.

- Inspired by how "together" your ex was, you now have concrete personal and professional goals that are serving you well.

Are you starting to see how the time you spent with your ex wasn't a total loss? By rewriting the good from your relationship with Mr. Wrong, as well as acknowledging the not-so-good (and the downright bad and ugly stuff), you start to create a clearer vision of your future. And while you don't need a new boyfriend to enjoy your life, by becoming increasingly specific about the kind of person you're looking to attract (someone so much better suited for you), you're able to move forward without getting sidetracked by the ghosts of your relationship past or yet another Mr. Wrong.

Bitter, Party of None

When a relationship ends, especially if it wasn't on your terms, it's easy to sink into despair, self-pity, and, ultimately, bitterness. So how can you tell if you're knee-deep in despair or up to your eyeballs in bitterness? If your current belief system goes something like this:

- All men are scum.
- I'm never letting anyone near my heart again.
- Love is a ridiculous illusion only suckers believe in.
- The next man I meet (and every man after him) is *so* going to pay for the sins of my ex.
- Men are lying, cheating bastards so I guess I'll give girls a try.

While it's perfectly normal to have any of the above beliefs randomly float through your head in the occasional bitter moment, if you've decided to permanently reside in Bitterness County, you're most likely headed for trouble. But before you write yourself off as a lost cause, stop. Back up. There's still hope.

Today and moving forward, you're going to instead become bitter, party of none. All you have to do to break free of your bitterness is to shift your focus from what could have been in the past to what will be in your future. So how do you do that? You start by practicing gratitude for your amazing life and its many gifts.

It may sound impossible, but it's not. It can be challenging, especially at first. I know that there are days when you feel like the world is against you. Days when it seems like you're the only single person on the planet, when everyone else is bliss-fully in love and you're starting over—for the first time or yet again. Even after healing and moving on from your ex, there are most likely still moments when his haunting presence feels almost suffocating. Or your focus on his amazing future keeps you from being able to create your own blissful future. Sound familiar?

These are the times when you need to practice gratitude the most. See, it's not about how amazing your life is. It's about how you feel about your amazing life, including the rough patches. Starting today, I invite you to practice gratitude for the simplest gifts in your everyday life. Make this one of your new rituals, something you do when you first wake up or right before you go to bed. Begin by saying *I am grateful for . . .* and then fill in the blank. Try to come up with at least five things every day that you're thankful for. The following are just a few examples of what you might give thanks for on a regular basis.

Your Health

While boyfriends come and go, career satisfaction shrinks and grows depending on the day, and unexpected life challenges present themselves and ultimately get resolved, nothing can give you peace of mind quite like enjoying a healthy mind and body. If you've been blessed with good health, give thanks. If you experience daily physical challenges, practice gratitude in the moments when you're feeling healthy and strong. When you feel weak, frail, or physically challenged, stay centered. Remind yourself that the feelings will pass. When the light at the end of the tunnel emerges (i.e., your health returns), celebrate it by giving thanks and expressing gratitude.

Your Family and Friends

If you're lucky enough to have an amazingly supportive network of friends and/or family members, give thanks. Not everyone is so lucky. And if your last breakup taught you anything, it's that you need a Boohoo Crew turned Woohoo Crew to see you through the tough times as well as to celebrate your successes. When in doubt about what to give thanks for, practice gratitude for the unconditional love you receive on a regular basis from your friends and family. While it may sometimes feel like you're all alone, you probably have a silent cheerleader or two rooting you on from the sidelines. Look for them, celebrate them, and give thanks for them.

Your Career

You may not be blessed with your dream job. And there are probably days you'd love to give your two weeks' notice. But the truth is, many people would be thankful to have the job you have. When in doubt, give thanks for being employed. If you find that you just can't practice gratitude about your career, it may be time to make a change. As you reinvent your life moving forward, start thinking about what kind of career would really rock your world. If you have the skill set, seek out a job change. If not, consider going back to school to get the career training or additional education you need. And again, give thanks that you have the smarts and ability to find and hold a job, get paid for your intelligence and skills, and that you have so many opportunities readily available.

Your Healing Heart

Here's something else to be grateful for: your breakup. Not so much the end of your relationship with your ex, but the strength and resilience you've discovered since the breakup happened. As your heart continues to heal, give thanks that the pain has subsided, that your ex is becoming more and more of a distant memory, and that day by day, you're learning valuable life lessons. Without the breakup, you wouldn't experience these gifts. Even if memories of your ex still seem far too fresh, go ahead and practice gratitude for your progress so far and commit to healing your heart as you move forward.

By practicing gratitude on a daily basis, you'll hopefully let go of any remaining bitterness about what could have been and instead firmly focus on your bright future. If you struggle with this exercise, don't worry. It's an ongoing process that takes patience, perseverance, and practice. With your ex behind you and your amazing life in front of you, I hope you'll make and take the time each day to celebrate all the amazing gifts you regularly receive.

1. What life experiences have you enjoyed so far or are you looking forward to, thanks to the fact that Mr. Ex is no longer in your life?

2. What wonderful, amazing, valuable lessons are you learning because of your ex?

3. To start practicing gratitude daily, ask yourself the following question: What are you grateful for? Make a list of at least five things. Continue adding to the list as you move forward.

chapter 3

one is *not* the loneliest number

Now that reality has set in—that you are a savvy and saucy single—what else is setting in? Fear, dread, and uncertainty about the future? Or excitement, inspiration, and hope? Chances are, you're experiencing a little bit of both right now—and that's perfectly normal. Whether you're suddenly single for the first time in a long time (or the first time ever!), or starting over at an age you never expected, this journey can be both exhilarating and excruciating. It can rock your world for better and worse. But before you let your single status capsize your entire life, tune into your internal compass in search of balance. Celebrate your single self for the amazing woman you are!

from the *fearless female files* . . .

"Sometimes things just aren't meant to be and you are able to really live your life to the fullest without that other person. As sad as it is, it's just true." —belinda

Newly Single, Party of One

There are many defining phases in a woman's life. Being single is one of them. Being seriously single for the first time is an exceptionally special one. When you move beyond the sheer terror of claiming your single status (perfectly normal), the undeniable panic that you may never meet someone again (so not true!), and the fear that often accompanies being minus a plus one at parties (we all experience that now and again), you begin to see how exciting life as a savvy single can be. Whereas once upon a time you defined yourself by the relationship you were in or the guy you were dating, you now have the opportunity to redefine who you are on your own two feet. If that idea causes you to break out in a cold sweat, chill. Take a breath. Keep reading.

No longer confined or constrained in a relationship with Mr. Wrong, you're now free to reinvent any and all areas of your life that no longer work for you.

Your Career

With the pain of your breakup behind you and your healing heart on the mend, you now have the good fortune of time, space, and energy to devote to professional pursuits. Want to land a promotion? Put some of your savvy skills to good use; take the lead on highly visible projects, share new ideas and solutions with your boss or team, and approach your daily work life with renewed enthusiasm. Chances are your efforts will be noticed and eventually pay off!

If you work for yourself, now's the time to rock your business by scoring a new client, educating yourself on your competitors and how you can provide added value, or launching a brand-new entrepreneurial endeavor.

At this unique time in your life, the sky's the limit when it comes to exploring exciting professional opportunities you may not have had the time or energy for during your last relationship.

from the *fearless female files* . . .

"My ex and I moved to Las Vegas a few years ago. Immediately, I just loved it! He did not. He was very jealous. As his rock, I felt the need to do what he did so he would feel comfortable. Eventually, I shut down. I couldn't be the person I was becoming. Getting out of that relationship, I got to be Nikki in Las Vegas, which is a beautiful thing. That led to networking with people, bringing more business to my company, and just enjoying being me. By staying with him, I just would have missed out on living." —nikki

Your Social Life

Now that you're footloose and fancy-free, how do you want to reinvent your social life? While it's true that you may spend the occasional Saturday night alone now that you're single, your social life shouldn't have to suffer just because your ex is no longer in the picture. What ridiculously fantastic activities do you want to incorporate into your routine? If you've got single friends, take turns organizing activities on the weekends including going out dancing, renting movies and staying in, attending singles' events, and putting yourself in target-rich environments on a regular basis.

What's a target rich environment? It's a location where the type of guy you're looking to attract can be found regularly—and in large numbers. For example, if you like live music, small music venues featuring live acts you enjoy are target-rich environments conducive to mingling and meeting (cute) live music fans. If you're passionate about art, scour the community guide in your local newspaper for upcoming art shows, museum benefits, and so on. Try to attend at least one art-related target rich function a month. And if you love the outdoors, join an outdoor-centric group like the Sierra Club and regularly attend their organized events. Even if you never make a love connection, it's a great way to meet new people while enjoying nature.

If you're the only single person in your social circle, now's the time to expand your horizons. Attend networking events, volunteer opportunities, or community activities where you can meet like-minded people, some of whom are bound to be single.

And no, you don't have to give up your happily hooked up-friends. You can still enjoy their company. But if your social interaction outside of work is limited to people who haven't been single in years whose conversations center around birthday parties with bouncy castles, you may start feeling like an outcast. And it's not like these friends have ill intentions. Well meaning as they are, they just can't relate to you and your single life. That's why you've got to find some single soul sisters. It's important to have a social circle that gets what you're going through and can celebrate your triumphs (getting hit on by that cutie you always see at Starbucks, that fantastic Friday night makeout session with Mr. Next, and finding the perfect third-date outfit) as well as commiserate over the occasional singles setback (your crush not returning your last call, the Internet date gone awry, finding your ex on Facebook with photos of the new girl in his life, and so on).

Your Home

They say every man's home is his castle. As the Queen of Your Castle, how do you want to reinvent your home now that you're on your own and free to redecorate as you like? If you and your ex lived together and you're now reinventing yourself and your once-shared space, it's essential that you give your home a much-needed makeover. Paint the walls vibrant colors. Get new furniture. Invest in making your home the ultimate bachelorette pad, complete with sexy sheets, cocktail glasses to toast to your new life, and plenty of bath salts, lotions, and potions to feel ultra feminine 24/7!

If after the breakup you were the one to relocate, how do you want to re-create your space so that your focus is firmly on your fab future? Be sure to surround yourself with art, imagery, and inspired objects that make you feel good. Build yourself a single gal shrine complete with affirmations, a vision board complete with images and words that inspire you to live your most authentic and blissful life, and any other accessories that will remind you how fabulous being single really is, (as well as what you'd like to manifest in your romantic future). Like a butterfly emerging from a cocoon, a new and improved you is unfolding day by day. Give her the space, nurturing, and opportunity to spread her beautiful wings and fly.

Become a Real Estate Mogul

Here's another way to rock your domestic reinvention: Invest in your first piece of property! Sound daunting? Think again. Millions of single women purchase property on their own. And while you may not initially get the sprawling digs complete with white picket fence, dog, and dream man that you once envisioned of your first home, purchasing a piece of property may be just the thing to help you rock your home life reinvention. So instead of getting hung up on the idea that you can't afford your mini mansion in the best neighborhood in town, remind yourself that you're just getting started. Maybe you begin by investing in a cute condo that's beach-adjacent. Maybe you and a friend or family member buy a home together in your fave neighborhood. Instead of simply believing, "I can't afford to buy a home on my own," ask a better question. For example, "*How* can I own my first home?" You might be surprised to discover that home ownership is absolutely and positively within your reach. Plus, when you *do* buy a home on your own, imagine how empowered, inspired, and proud you'll be of your single self!

Your Mind/Body/Spirit

Be honest. Does being single sometimes feel like a life sentence? Does it feel like something you have to endure indefinitely, hopelessly suffering through, in hopes of one day getting real relief when Mr. Right shows up? If you answered yes, don't beat yourself up. Millions of single women who have come before you have felt the exact same way. And when they were introduced to a saucy little secret via their fellow females, everything changed.

Want to know that secret?

The key to unlocking your prison cell is to free yourself. Sound corny? Keep reading. Start by celebrating who you are right this very minute, learning to nurture your mind, body, and spirit. And no, you don't have to be a Zen master to achieve this. Simply start by tuning in to your internal thoughts, feelings, and beliefs on a daily basis. Listen to your inner dialogue. If you notice repeated negative beliefs, see if you can reframe them into more positive ones. For example, if you constantly find yourself thinking *I hate being single* or *When it comes to love, everyone else seems to get it right. Why can't I?*, ask a better question. For example, shift from *I hate being single* to *What can I do today to enjoy being single more?* The answers that come may surprise you. And the subtle shifts that follow can do wonders for your outlook on your single-and-ready-to-mingle life.

Now's also the perfect time to explore your spirituality. If you're religiously inclined, deepen that connection to your deity by going to church, meditating, or participating in other spiritual practices. If you're new to spirituality but interested in deepening your experience, start reading everything you can about what interests you. Invest in books and online research. Attend seminars and workshops. Let your internal compass guide you toward the spiritual practices that most speak to you. In doing so, you give yourself permission to flourish as a spiritual being. Plus, you're going to meet interesting, like-minded, and open-minded individuals who will shape your journey and may lead you in new and exciting directions. Go ahead, explore!

A New Passion

Do you have a deep-seeded desire that's never quite come to light? Is there something you're secretly passionate about, yet until now that passion has been lying dormant and unexplored? From a lurking hobby to an internal compass-directed passion, now is your chance to step aside and let your true desires unfold. Everyone's personal passion is different. It can be as simple as knowing you want to go back to school but feeling afraid to go for it. Or hearing a small voice inside telling you it's time to switch careers. Or maybe you've always had a fascination with the ocean and would secretly love to get certified as a scuba diver, but have never expressed it out of fear, doubt, or insecurity. Don't worry about how you'll look in a wetsuit. Just go for it!

What are you waiting for? One of the most exquisite gifts being single affords you is the opportunity to call all the shots. You decide how your money gets spent, what you give your time and energy to, and how you live your life. Sometimes having so much choice can feel overwhelming. But the truth is that your freedom is a gift. Don't squander it, convinced it's a burden. Cherish it. Celebrate it! Give yourself permission to become that amazing woman you secretly know you are. This is your chance to be self-indulgent and self-nurturing (not to mention bold). What are you waiting for?

The Unexpected Single

If you're starting over at an age you never expected, regardless of what that age is, the good news is, you're in good company. I have worked with hundreds of women who found themselves starting over at an age they once thought would be defined by marriage, babies, and possibly a summer home someplace fabulous. Instead, like you, they had to pick up the pieces, redefine themselves, and re-create their future—on their own two feet.

Sound daunting? That's because it is. But it's also one of the best gifts you can give yourself: The opportunity to move on from a life that for whatever reason no longer works into a life full of possibility. Think about all those scared, stagnant, uncertain women stuck in dead-end relationships wishing they had the strength and courage to start all over again. You're their hero. More importantly, you're your own hero. Now's the time to start acting like it.

So what's a heroine to do?

Rock her reinvention, of course! Instead of cowering in some corner for the next six months apologizing for being single, or worse, holding onto your identity as *what's his name's* girlfriend/fiancée/wife even though your ex is long gone, today's the day to celebrate your suddenly single status and start asking yourself these very important questions:

- What do I want to do now?
- Who do I want to become now?
- What exciting, exhilarating, unbelievable opportunities await me now that I'm free to explore them?

Whether you know it or not, your reinvention has already begun. And you're doing perfectly. Moment by moment, day by day, you're getting stronger, more confident, and tuning in to that small voice inside who's guiding you into your future. Your only job right now is to pay attention, follow her lead, and turn down the volume on those other, negative voices. They couldn't be more wrong. Your happily ever after is unfolding as we speak. It's up to you to bring it to life.

Facebook Friends Weigh In

When asked the question *When it comes to reinventing your life following a breakup, what were some of the challenges and blessings you experienced?* on Facebook, here's what some of my fab friends said. . . .

"That my ex wasn't really right for me to begin with. Once I let him go, my life got so much better! A new job, a new hairstyle, and the chance to really be me." —GINA

"Once I realized that my life wasn't over, I started having fun again. Saturday nights with my girls, brunch with friends, and time to myself. I loved every minute of it!" —KAREN

"Living alone was hard at first. Feeling like no one would care where I was or what I was doing or if I was okay. That got easier in time." —SARAH

In order for you to do that, you need to be really honest with yourself by summoning the courage to take an honest look at your last relationship and past relationships. Now's the time to do some important emotional excavation work. Start asking yourself some questions. They can include:

- How did I participate in both the good and bad in my past relationships?
- How was my ex both right and wrong for me?
- What lessons have I learned from my life and love history? How can I apply them to my future?
- What do I now know I want in life and love?

Really take some time to ask and answer these questions. As challenging as it might seem at first, it's essential to your future that you perform this emotional excavation. It's not always going to be fun. But what you unearth will inform your happily-ever-after future in ways you never would have expected. You owe it to yourself to do the work so you can re-create, re-envision, and reinvent your savvy single self and that future you're working toward.

from the *fearless female files* . . .

"When I was newly single, I didn't know what to do with myself. First of all, I didn't have any friends to call. I had been pretty much quarantined during the relationship. And it felt scary to start over and go out on my own. I thought, 'How am I going to meet people? What am I going to do?' Then I got over it. I realized, 'Wait a minute. I can do this!' I started going out and meeting the most amazing people! For a moment, just the threat of loneliness, the threat of, 'I'm all alone, just me and the cat.' It was paralyzing but then I woke up, remembered who I was, and decided to get on with things."—monica

Constant Contact

During this new process, you'll want to not only turn down the volume on your inner critic who tells you all those evil, awful, judgmental things about who you are, what you deserve, and what your future looks like, but you'll also want to create some new constants for yourself. Your new constants will re-inform your beliefs about where you're going and what you deserve.

They may look something like this:

- I deserve a happily-ever-after future.
- I forgive myself for my past and look forward to my future.
- Real and lasting love is possible for me. Every day, I get closer to it.
- I commit to my own happiness and find ways to celebrate my life on a daily basis.
- God wants me to be in a loving, lifelong relationship.

Identify key words and phrases that are important to you and incorporate them into your new set of constants. If you're still in a place of crying over the past or wondering if your ex was your perfect partner and without him you feel lost, pick at least one constant that reminds you why it's good he's gone.

Again, don't skip over this exercise. Creating new constants will be your beacon in times of uncertainty. Whenever your inner critic rears his ugly head, stop, take a deep breath, and review your constants.

Having trouble creating your constants? I've compiled a list of some of my favorite constants that my clients have shared with me over the years. Feel free to borrow from or be inspired by the list. . . .

1. He wasn't there for me when I needed him the most if it wasn't convenient for him . . . do I really want this?
2. He has been selfish for 90 percent of the relationship. This will *never* change.

3. I deserve someone who celebrates me just as I am and doesn't belittle me.
4. He sold me a false product (who he claimed he was versus who he really is) and I'm a pissed off customer.
5. I am a catch and my perfect partner will be lucky to catch me!

The Bachelorette Lifestyle

Now that you've reclaimed your space, embraced the endless possibilities unfolding in front of you, and re-created your constants, the fun can begin! It's time to become the ultimate bachelorette. And no, I'm not talking about staging your own reality show, having weekly rose ceremonies, and falling in faux love by next Tuesday. I'm talking about celebrating your single self like never before. *How* you do this isn't important. What's important is that you find your own personal spin on becoming the ultimate bachelorette. Will you:

1. Channel your inner Samantha Jones and juggle men like a pro?
2. Redecorate your home in warm, sexy, lush colors, textures, and prints so that any man who walks through the front door will immediately fall under your saucy spell?
3. Throw weekly cocktail parties for your Woohoo Crew, groove to girl-power music, and celebrate your fabulous single selves?
4. Undergo a major physical transformation, losing 15 pounds, changing your hair color, and splurging on a sassy new wardrobe?

5. Trade in your worn wheels for a bachelorette mobile, complete with convertible top, pink racing stripe, and leather seats (perfect for picking up cuties while flirting in traffic!)?

In embracing the ultimate bachelorette lifestyle, the goal isn't to become someone you're not. Instead, you simply want to make space for the most awesome version of yourself to emerge. While being single can sometimes feel suffocating, your job right now is to find meaningful ways to celebrate it and just have fun. If the idea of pimping your wheels, home, or wardrobe feels unattainable, start smaller. Get that sexy new 'do. Sign up for speed dating. Or commit to putting yourself in a target-rich environment once a week so you can practice making eye contact, smiling, and saying hello. Before you know it, your very best bachelorette self will emerge and start turning heads wherever she goes. Again, remember that this is a process. It doesn't happen overnight. Practice patience, push your comfort zone, and honor your heart. And of course, have fun!

1. Now that you're free to reinvent any and all areas of your life that no longer work for you, what area needs your attention first? Create an action plan for moving forward.

2. If you're single at an age you never expected, start asking and answering these questions:

   A. What do I want to do now?

   B. Who do I want to become now?

   C. What exciting, exhilarating, unbelievable opportunities await me now that I'm free to explore them?

3. To help you move forward fearlessly, create your new set of constants. See examples on page 44–45 for reference.

Let's Talk!

I invite you to share your ahas! with me on my Facebook fan page. Go to Facebook.com and search for my fan page.

chapter 4

fairytales do come true (and other lies your mother told you)

Now that you've figured out just how fabulous being single versus staying in the wrong relationship is, identified life lessons from your last love, and are practicing gratitude daily, it's time to travel once again into the past. Only this time, I want you to go *way* back—to your childhood.

What were some of the earliest messages you got about love, marriage, and relationships? And not just from watching your parents' relationship. Think about your collective childhood influences when it came to romance. From the fairytales your parents read you at bedtime to the Disney movies you adored that promised a happy ending, to the songs, television shows, and big-screen romances that told you love conquers all, it probably never occurred to your little-girl brain that some of those messages were, well, lies.

Even though the school of life has taught you differently you may still buy into some of those childhood fantasies as an adult. Now's the time to debunk the myths, fables, and fairytales that just might be sabotaging your chances of a realistic happily-ever-after future. Like it or not, you can't call in Mr. Right (or even Mr. Next) without first letting go of Prince Charming. So slip on your big-girl slippers and let's get to work!

Someday My Prince Will Come (Back)

Be honest. Are you still holding out hope that your ex may one day come back, sweep you off your feet, give you everything you ever wanted, and radically change everything about himself that didn't work in your relationship? From getting his act together financially to learning how to be emotionally available 24/7 to loudly and proudly proclaiming his love for you in front of everyone he knows, are you putting your future on hold, praying for a miracle? Have you put in a good effort in your post-breakup recovery, even going so far as to create a cute online dating profile, go out on a few first dates, but deep down, you're waiting for the phone to ring or your ex to show up on your front doorstep with flowers, a ring, and a marriage proposal?

Remember, I said be honest.

The good news is you wouldn't be the first woman in history to put her fabulous future on hold in the hope that with a little time, distance, and perspective, her ex would magically discover the error of his ways, come running back, and together, they'd live happily ever after.

The bad news is that while you're fantasizing about your happily-ever-after reunion with your ex, he's moving on without you. He's dating other women. Even if he's still calling you.

And, yes, even if he's still sleeping with you.

While it's debatable whether or not men and women are actually from different planets, as John Gray would have us believe, the painful truth is this: Men and women handle break-ups differently. Yes, we both mourn in our own way. Yes, we both feel grief, loss, disappointment—in our own way. But many men can stay connected to their exes throughout their recovery and still move on while most women cannot.

And while some couples do part ways, recognize the error of their ways, and reunite to create a brand new healthy, happy future, the more realistic reality is that while you're snuggling in your ex's arms after yet another night of late night passion (also known as the post-breakup booty call), he's still moving on with his life. He's still making other plans. He's still dating other people. And while he likes the comfort of falling back into bed with you, he still believes you're broken up for good because, well, you are.

If any of the above rings true, don't fool yourself into thinking you're the exception to the rule. If you're reading this book, you're looking for answers. And I'm going to give them to you whether you really want to hear them or not.

If the bestselling book *He's Just Not That into You* taught us anything, it's that you're not the exception. You're the rule.

Let me clarify that. If you're still in constant communication with your ex or enjoying the occasional or frequent reunion between the sheets, stop. This is not a sign you're getting back together. It's not even a sign he's still in love with you. While you may still be madly in love with him, he's moving on without you. You're his emotional airbag, providing support and security as he slowly but surely re-enters the dating world. It doesn't work in reverse. He's not your airbag. He's the accident waiting to happen that will destroy you (which is exactly how you'll feel when you discover he's dating someone else). The *really* infuriating part? He's not even leading you on! You're leading yourself on.

How? By silently agreeing to stay connected. By giving him your body, thinking he's giving you his heart. By taking his calls, thinking that means you're the only woman he's talking to these days. And even if you are right this minute, who's to say he won't meet someone tomorrow, continue to see both of you until things get serious with the other woman, and then one day he'll show up on your doorstep, hand you a box of things you left at his place, and tell you he's madly in love with the new lady in his life and they're engaged. Ouch! (That's a true story from the dating trenches.)

Think your ex is above such heartless behavior? Think again. These post-breakup tactics are not limited to jerks, assholes, and players. Good men, honest men, kind men, men like your ex do this because you *let* them. Because on some level you accept his behavior. You say it's okay because you still love him. You silently agree to be nothing more than a booty call because your heart tells you it's better than being nothing to your ex. Maybe you can't have the relationship you once had, but you can still hold onto your ex in some tiny way. Yes, it's painful, but it's also comfortable, familiar, and it means you don't have to take any risks. Risks like walking away and focusing on your future. Risks like giving your heart to someone else. Risks like cutting your ex out of your life completely.

You couldn't be more wrong.

Maybe men and women are from different planets. But unlike the fair and balanced relationships women like to have on Venus, on Mars it's perfectly acceptable to sleep with your ex, date someone new, fall in love, and kick your ex to the curb once things get serious. Ouch!

So what's a savvy gal like you to do? For starters, wake up and smell the reality. Second, wise up and stop letting your ex back into your life. In fact, get rid of everything that reminds you of him, including old photos, his t-shirt you're still secretly sleeping in, and any remaining connections to him online. You know what I'm talking about, Facebook lurker!

In doing so, you take your power back. You also take an important step into your more realistic future. Guess what else? In stepping beyond the invisible electric fence your ex has had around your heart, you create the space for someone new and amazing to come into your life, when you're ready. Woohoo!

Now, I think I've done a pretty good job of illustrating the dangers of staying connected to your ex or holding out hope for one last reunion. But let's review one last time. Regardless of how many times you've broken up and gotten back together, thought you were meant to be, and/or still compare every guy you meet to your ex, it's time for a serious reality check. If you're putting your future on hold indefinitely, how long are you willing to wait? How much more time are you willing to waste? And what's it going to take for you to completely disconnect your heart from your ex?

Right here and now, I invite you to walk away for good. I know it's scary. The big, bad unknown future is out there in front of you. But isn't it time you explored it by cutting off all ties to your ex, including the emotional ones? Today, give yourself permission to stop looking over your shoulder waiting for him to come back one last time and instead commit to yourself and what lies ahead for you.

The Curse of "The One"

Now that your ex is gone, there are other lingering emotional saboteurs that may need to be exorcised. Sure, you've given up the ghost of your ex, but what about the curse of The One? Is that another lie your mother or society told you growing up that needs to be set straight? It is if you're clinging to any of the following beliefs:

I know there's just one perfect person for me. My soul mate! My everything!

Where is The One? What's taking him so long? Hurry up!

My happy ending is just around the corner. I don't have to do anything but sit here and wait for Mr. Right to show up.

If this sounds familiar, it's time for another serious reality check.

Let's get real. *If* there is only one perfect person in the world for you, what are the chances of ever finding each other? With billions of people on the planet, even with the power of the Internet, what are the odds that you and this one amazing man will find one another before you're eighty and in a retirement home? And, let's just say you're lucky enough to live in the same state, city, and zip code as this perfect catch. What's the likelihood of running into one another randomly at a coffee house, wine bar, or speed dating event, recognizing one another as The One, and instantly falling head over heels? Slim to none?

Slim, meet None.

Here's what's wrong with the whole notion that there's only one person ideally suited for you in the entire world: It's too limiting! Maybe your mother's generation, or even your grandmother's generation, needed to believe in "The One" because it made settling down with the first guy who courted her, proposed to her, and rescued her from a life of spinsterhood seem romantic. After all, in the 1950s a woman had extremely limited options available to her. With minimal career choices (secretary, teacher, and nurse), women rarely lived alone, let alone bought property on their own. It made sense that a single woman in the 1950s needed to hold out hope for Prince Charming, The White Knight, or The One to come along, sweep her off her feet, and provide her happily-ever-after ending.

In those days, maybe a husband really *did* rescue a woman from her life. Gave her a home, paid the bills, fathered her children, and, if she was lucky, treated her with love and respect. Today you don't need to be someone's wife to have a roof over your head, a checking account, or a home of your own. You have the luxury of being able to provide all that for yourself.

Let's re-check your reality. If you're still holding tight to some notion that Mr. Right is out there just waiting patiently to find you, that your relationship is predestined in the stars, or that one day in the not too distant future, some guy will show up on your front doorstep, introduce himself as "The One," and then the two of you can finally get on with your blissful life—stop right there. You're not Sleeping Beauty or Cinderella. It's time to wake up and burst that limiting (not to mention infuriating) bubble that says you're supposed to wait around for some guy who's never going to show up because he doesn't exist. You, my savvy single friend, are far too fabulous to be kept waiting by any man, let alone a figment of fairytales. Now's the time to cast aside your rose-colored glasses, don a fabulous pair of designer shades, and jump into the twenty-first century with both feet! The truth is there are tons of awesome, amazing, handsome, eclectic, intelligent, creative, driven, delightful single men in the world just dying to meet someone like you. But until you break free from the captivating spell of a fairytale ending, you aren't ready, willing, or able to spot them. Even if you were, they wouldn't be interested in you because you're hopelessly hooked on outdated ideas about love and relationships.

That is, until five seconds ago, right? Now that you know better, you're going to retrain your brain and behave accordingly. Consider this book your brand new dating bible. Out of the ashes you will rise not bruised and battered from mistakes of the past or hung up on unrealistic beliefs about The One, but stronger, more centered, and more authentically you than ever before. You're in it to win it, and that means celebrating the fact that you're not on the lookout for The One anymore, but The One Sitting Next to You at the Sushi Bar, or The One Volunteering for Your Favorite Cause Alongside You, or The One Smiling at You Across the Room at Your Fave Music Lounge. And now that you know they're everywhere, it's up to you to spot these potential Ones, shoot them a sassy smile, and see what happens next. Does this mean you're making the first move? No. It means you're giving the guy a green light to make the first move. Once you grant him permission, if he's smart he'll take the initiative and go for it!

The Bad Boy with a Heart of Gold

Here's another maddening myth that needs debunking right now. Are you addicted to bad boys? You are if you've spent years chasing guys who weren't interested in you, convinced that one day they'd magically transform from an emotionally unavailable frog into a sweet and sensitive prince.

You are not alone here. In fact, let me give you an example from my own life. I still clearly remember watching *Grease* as a kid. I marveled at how beautiful Olivia Newton John looked in her poodle skirts and sweater sets. I was hooked on how handsome John Travolta was in his black leather. And when Danny and Sandy's rocky relationship suddenly became a fairy-tale reunion at the end of the film, my seven-year-old heart pounded with glee. True love really *did* conquer all! Plus, my chubby pre-tween self couldn't wait to look as good as Sandy did in those skintight black leggings (I'm still waiting!). But here's the part I *really* remember. As my mother and I stood up to leave the theater when the end credits rolled, my mother turned to me and said, "In real life, he'd change for her."

Oh no she didn't!

Oh yes she did.

Is it any wonder I chased emotionally unavailable bad boys throughout my teens and twenties, waiting for them to change their ways, convinced I could make them love me? My mother wasn't intentionally trying to mislead me about love and relationships. She really believed what she was saying. It's just that she, too, was raised on fairytales. And until I broke free from my own bad boy addiction (which I eventually did), there was no way I could experience real and lasting love.

So the question remains. Are you addicted to bad boys, expecting them to change their ways for you? And if so, how's that working out? How many times have you fallen for some guy who just wasn't into you, invested too much time, and barely escaped with a tattered heart and bruised ego?

It's time once and for all to face facts. Bad boys are called that for a reason. They're B-A-D for your heart, your head, your emotions, and your ego. Emotionally unavailable guys are downright infuriating. And a frog is still a frog, even if he's a fantastic kisser. (Don't worry. In Chapter 11, I'll talk all about the boys to avoid, and how to eventually make room for a really nice guy who will make your heart beat faster without the accompanying bad boy nausea.)

And They Lived Unhappily Ever After

With the slide of a glass slipper onto a dainty foot, Prince Charming fell in love with Cinderella. Sleeping Beauty was rescued by a magical kiss from Prince Phillip. And after years of single-girl solitude, Rapunzel met her dashing prince when he climbed her lengthy and lustrous hair and freed her from a life of captivity.

Fast-forward to the new millennium. When Cinderella flees The House of Blues at midnight without explanation, Prince Charming doesn't pick up her shoe and wistfully long for the girl who's gone. Instead, he whips out his iPhone, dials a few digits, and arranges a booty call with one of her evil stepsisters. And Sleeping Beauty? Her prince capitalizes on her narcolepsy, surfing the web for porn, eating all her food, and drinking all her beer. As for Rapunzel? Her hair extensions eventually fall out and the Prince stops calling because he just wasn't that into her.

Let's face it. In the twenty-first century, being single can be brutal. That's why it's essential to your happily-ever-after future that you free yourself from the fairytale trap and any other ridiculous rescue fantasies you may be holding onto. These fantasies go something like this. . . .

I don't have to pay off my debt/invest in my retirement/buy a home on my own. My husband, wherever he is, will provide that for me when he finally comes along.

Sure there are things I don't like about myself, but you know what? When my dream man gets here, all of that will magically disappear. So why put in the effort now?

All the guys I meet and date are losers. Where's my White Knight? That one perfect guy just for me. . . .

There's a reason relationship coaches call this kind of thinking the fairytale trap—because it's unrealistic, unhealthy, and totally toxic. And if you're trapped in it, you're screwed (until you get un-stuck, of course!). By putting off personal accountability, by *not* taking responsibility for your behavior and actions, and by subscribing to the belief that one day some guy will just come along and rescue you from your miserable life, your fairytale ending is looking pretty grim.

But don't worry. There's an end to your suffering. All you've got to do is free yourself from the fairytale trap. Start by taking an honest look at what you're putting off in your life, waiting for a man to provide. Do you expect a guy to bring financial security? Are you living beyond your means, hung up on the idea that the right guy will swoop in and fix your finances? Or, are there emotional issues in your life that you're not willing to face because you think they're temporary and when your perfect partner arrives, they'll magically disappear?

Life is not a fairytale. You've got to face yourself, your demons, and your shortcomings head on—starting today! By taking steps to become your best self, to free yourself from unhealthy emotional beliefs, and to really celebrate the beautiful woman inside of you, quirks and all, you position yourself to one day meet someone really special. However, if you choose to stay stuck in dysfunction, limiting beliefs, and poor emotional health, the likelihood of meeting and wooing some-one amazing dramatically drops. The choice is yours. Stay stuck in a fairytale fantasy, or face the sometimes-harsh realities of life head on with humility, grace, and strength. Now's the time to take steps toward a healthier, happier, more realistic future.

After reading this chapter, how do you feel? Enlightened and ready to face your future with a more realistic approach to love and relationships? Or frustrated, hopeless, and with a sense of dread? The goal here wasn't to burst your bubble (okay, maybe it was). It was to educate you so that you can approach dating and relationships with clarity, hope, and wisdom. Be sure to answer the questions in the chapter review to further revise your belief system.

1. What, if any, fairytales do you subscribe to? How might they be sabotaging your chances at real love?

2. How can you start incorporating a more realistic view of love and relationships into your belief system?

3. If you're stuck in the fairytale trap, how can you free yourself, starting today? Create an action plan and start implementing it.

Added Support Getting Freedom from Fairytales

Need help letting go of fairytales and other traps? E-mail me your questions at *ask@LisaSteadman.com*.

chapter 5

stuck, stuck, loose!

Now that your last relationship is fading into the distance, you may be wondering what's next for you. While you've most likely learned some valuable lessons from your relationship history, and may even look to your dating future with optimism, possibility, and hope, how do you guarantee better love next time? Not only that, but how do you keep from merely repeating the same relationship mistakes with someone new, and instead experience different (and happier) results? Most important, how do you cut down on wasted time in the dating trenches with Mr. Wrong, easily and effortlessly making room for Mr. Next (and eventually Mr. Right)?

The key to your successful dating future lies in your ability to learn quickly, adapt to change, and ultimately avoid getting stuck in the myriad of dating pitfalls on the journey from *Boohoo!* to *Woohoo!* What follows are some of the most common ways women waste days, weeks, months, and even years of their fabulous lives in the wrong relationship or between relationships. See which pitfalls you fall prey to, and what you can do to get un-stuck.

from the *fearless female files* . . .

"I was in a relationship with someone that made me feel so low, I didn't have the strength to leave, even though I told myself I should. He was the one who ended it. At first I was upset with myself for not leaving him sooner. I have since realized him leaving was my only way out."—laura

Pitfall #1: You Stay Too Long in the Wrong Relationship

Be honest. Have you ever stayed too long in the wrong relationship? Or—gulp—do you chronically stick around much longer than you know you should, only to later regret wasted time, energy, and unhappiness? If you fall into either of these camps, don't beat yourself up. You're actually in excellent (and crowded) company. Truthfully, most women stay too long in the wrong relationship at least once, if not repeatedly.

Why?

In my coaching practice, I have come to understand the most common reasons women get and choose to stay stuck (yes, they actually make a choice to stay there). See which ones resonate most with you.

Reason #1:
You're Afraid No One Else Will Come Along

Far too many fabulous women stay in the wrong relationship because they secretly fear that what they've got is as good as it gets. As much as these amazing women would like to believe real and lasting love exists with their perfect partner, feelings of fear and uncertainty are so overpowering that they convince themselves it's better to stay with the guy they've got than to risk being single and alone.

This is especially common as women get older. Once they reach their late thirties, forties, and even fifties, women often fall prey to the scarcity myth that there are no good men left so if she's dating someone or in a relationship, she's lucky to have a man, regardless of how he treats her. The problem with this limited thinking is that these same women decide that while the relationship they're in isn't exactly what they'd hoped for, it's better than nothing. And rather than digging deep, summoning that inner strength, and getting unstuck from Mr. Wrong, they spend years (decades even!) in the wrong relationship, trying to make it work but feeling increasingly frustrated, unsatisfied, and, well, stuck.

The results? Living a life in limbo. Constantly questioning "Is he The One?" all the while, deep down, knowing the answer's "No." (Not to mention never meeting someone better suited for them because they're already spoken for!)

If and when these women *do* leave (or if and when the guy leaves them—unfortunately, a more likely outcome), they kick themselves for having stayed so long. It's an unhealthy lose-lose scenario women corner themselves into. And if this sounds familiar, you, too, have been buying into a limited belief that does nothing more than keep you trapped in a so-so relationship.

Is this any way to live? No. But millions of incredibly smart, successful, savvy women live this way, all because it's too scary, unknown, and uncertain to move on, especially if all their friends are married with children and completely oblivious to the plight of the single gal.

from the *fearless female files* . . .

"I stayed in my last relationship too long because things felt right in the present, but he just didn't see a future with me. He always said he 'wasn't sure,' but that he couldn't see his future without me either. It was like being stuck in limbo. For a long time, my situation was too good to leave, but also too uncertain to stay. In the end I kind of forced a talk about our future (before I was about to quit my job and uproot my life to move to Seattle to be with him). He told me he couldn't continue the relationship anymore. I didn't resist or beg for him to stay or anything because I figured if I had to convince him I was right for him, I actually wasn't. He walked out the door and that was it."—tanya

Don't be that girl. Instead, summon your inner strength, ask for what you want, need, and desire, and if and when all signs point to Dump the Chump, act accordingly. And no, I'm not advocating breakups for all. But at some point you have to ask yourself *Is this relationship working?* And when you've done all you can to try to make it work and it's still not working (and your man's not willing to change, adapt, or grow), you need to face facts. Like or not, you cannot perform miracles. Relationships are a two-way street and when one of you isn't willing to participate in growth and improvement you both suffer the consequences. If the relationship as it is works for your partner but doesn't work for you, don't waste years in indecision. Act as quickly as possible and move on. Your happily-ever-after future depends on it!

Reason #2:
You Get Hung Up on His "Potential"

Here's another reason women get stuck in the wrong relationship. As the people-pleasing, caretaking individuals we are, we cut our partners a lot of slack. While that can be a great quality in the right relationship, in the wrong one it can be a burden—and a blindfold. By focusing far too much on a man's potential, and ignoring who he actually is, you sabotage your ability to make educated decisions about what's possible in the relationship, not to mention what your partner is truly capable of. To give you a better idea of what I mean, how many times have you or someone you know said any of the following:

He's got such a good heart. If only he could get his act together.

He's still figuring out what he wants to do with his life. Once he does, he'll get on track.

When things are good between us, our relationship is amazing. When it's not? He's very . . . challenging.

Things would be perfect if . . . (Fill in the blank: *If he'd open up to me, If he'd let go of his insecurities, If he'd stop being so critical of me,* and so on.)

Or, how often have you (or someone you know) put up with a guy's "quirks" even though deep down you know they were actually deal breakers? Things like:

- He says he's really into you but he just won't sleep with you.
- He swears he loves you but he insults you, demeans you, and/or verbally abuses you on a regular basis.
- He claims to want a future with you but he can't get his act together financially, let alone commit to moving in together, getting engaged, or setting a wedding date.
- He promises you're his number-one priority but everything else comes before you, including work, video games, his buddies, and his dog.

Let's be clear. Cutting the wrong guy way too much slack does nothing more than cut down on *your* chances of ever experiencing true relationship success. Yes, it's important to be open-minded, understanding, and realistic. But if you spend your entire dating and relationship life making excuses for why some guy can't or won't marry you, how his childhood ruined him forever and what he really needs is patience and understanding, or why it's *your* job to save him, you are in for a rude awakening, not to mention a bumpy ride.

The tough love truth is this. If some guy is stringing you along, never meeting you half way, and in general not making himself emotionally available to you. . . .

- He doesn't feel the same way about you that you feel about him.
- He's not your equal.
- He's never going to marry you.

- He will never want to have children with you.
- Not to be corny, but he's just not into you!

Not only that, but you are going to carry him—emotionally and/or financially—for the rest of your relationship. And don't romanticize that idea. It's hard work. Plus, it's draining and will most likely keep you from doing what you need to do with your life. If you've decided that's the road you want to take? Good luck. But before you travel too far down that road, take a long hard look at the path you're choosing. Make sure you're up for the sacrifice. And ask yourself this:

Is he worth it?

And don't answer like a burdened martyr who has to shoulder the inadequacies of the man she loves. Answer as the authentic, strong, amazing, independent woman you really are.

One more thing before you make your final decision about whether to stick it out or throw in the towel with Mr. Maybe (he's not even worthy of Mr. Next status). A guy who blames his misfortunes and commitment issues on a horrible childhood, an awful boss, or some ex girlfriend who ruined him for life is so not interesting, sexy, or worthy of your sympathy. There are plenty of happy, healthy, and emotionally available men in the world who may or may not have had difficult upbringings. They're just not shouting it from the rooftops. Instead, they're living functional lives as grown-up men who have let go of their need to blame someone else for what happened once upon a time, and are emotionally stable and ready to have a real relationship. Now *that* is a man worthy of your time, energy, and attention (and a potential candidate for Mr. Right!). But if you're too busy taking care of some head case or drama king, you will never be available to meet these fantastic catches. Your loss!

---

from the *fearless female files* . . .

"I was in a relationship with an undercover FBI agent. I found out he was deeply undercover in our relationship as well, posing as someone faithful and loving. He was a jerk before I found out he was cheating, but I kept going until I'd had enough. I didn't confront him about his betrayals as he would have denied it. Instead, I packed my things and got ready to leave under his 'detective' nose. He was so full of himself he didn't realize what I was doing. When I was ready (hardest week of my life), I sent him off to work, called my friend and she met me in a parking lot where I transferred all my things into her car. I left a short little note and was *gone* forever. It was the most empowering thing I have ever done."—trish

---

Although Trish's reaction—to sneak away—may seem a bit drastic, it's a reality for many women. If this is you, don't be ashamed! You are standing up for yourself.

Reason #3:
You Think You're Too Old to Start Over Again

In my coaching practice, I work with women of all ages. However, there's a significant percentage of women in their forties and fifties who seek me out because they worry that time has run out on their chance to ever experience real and lasting love. Some of the commonalities they share are that they have spent a lifetime putting everyone else's needs before their own. Many of them married young. They had children young. Along the way, they got divorced. They became single mothers. And at some point, they fell into an on-again, off-again relationship with a man who was emotionally unavailable, spiritually wounded, and/or in some other way not their equal. They never married, never lived together, and by the time these women reach out to me, they're D-O-N-E with the drama. They're also on the verge of having an empty nest. Truthfully, they're in panic mode. The kids are grown. The ex is gone—for good this time. And here they are, at forty-nine, fifty-four, or fifty-seven, single and alone.

It's terrifying!

But guess what else it is? Absolutely freakin' fabulous! Because as late as these women perceive they are in blooming, they are finally ready to make the conscious choice to put their own needs first. They're finally ready to say "Yes! I deserve that life I've only ever dreamed about before! Yes, I'm ready for real and lasting love. And along the way to my new vision of *happily ever after*, I'm going to date, love myself, and re-create a life I love."

The results are always remarkable. Handsome, interesting, and available men appear from all directions. New career opportunities present themselves. Beautiful self-love and self-awareness blossom. It's such a pleasure to witness these women emerging from their well-worn cocoons to become the brilliant butterflies they're meant to be!

Think you're too old to start over? Think again.

The truth is it's never too late to re-create your happily ever after, whether you're twenty-five, thirty-one, forty-three, fifty-five, or sixty! Rather than put it off any longer—say for another six months, six years, or (gulp!) forever by staying with Mr. Wrong—why not start your new life today? It's not as scary as it may seem. And by taking one step in the direction of the life you know you'd like to live if you could just get out of your own way and live it, you get that much closer to actually manifesting it. Plus, you change the kind of person who's attracted to your lifestyle, and ultimately call in potential partners who could one day become your perfect partner. Love that!

Pitfall #2: You Spend Too Much Time Trying to Get Your Ex Back

Here's another dangerous pitfall where many women find themselves capsizing and getting stuck along the journey toward happily ever after. Even after the breakup happens, many women fall prey to the hopeful notion that their ex might magically change his ways, do an emotional U-turn, and proclaim his undying love.

Here's what's wrong with this scenario. By constantly looking over your shoulder at the past, wondering if there's still hope, worrying whether your ex has already moved on, and in general postponing your life because your focus is in the wrong place, you guarantee only one result—staying stuck. And that's no way to live your life.

One of the reasons so many women stay stuck in the waiting, wondering, and wishing their ex would come back is this:

They think the best relationship, love, and connection they'll ever experience with a man is now in their past. They believe that even though things weren't perfect in the relationship, their ex must have been The One, that he knew them better than anyone else, and that the connection they felt was so special and electric that they will never again experience it with someone else.

Sound familiar?

If you answered no, congratulations. You just dodged a serious Staying Stuck bullet. If you answered yes, don't stress.

The good news is you're wrong. The bad news is that staying stuck in this pitfall is a choice. As the mistress of your destiny, it's up to you to choose to free yourself from this limited thinking. But until you change your belief system, putting real and lasting love, deep connection, and passion with staying power in your future, it will remain where it is—in your past.

Rather than waste any more of your time, energy, or emotions staring into the relationship rearview mirror, do yourself a huge favor. Make a list of all the traits, qualities, experiences, and attributes from past relationships that you loved, cherished, appreciated, and adored. Go ahead, make a list now or during the chapter review. Take an inventory of what you want to repeat from previous relationships in your next relationship. Things like . . .

1. Uncontrollable giggle fits just because you're having so much fun together.
2. Mood music, a bottle of wine, and spending time together in the kitchen cooking.
3. Someone to stroke your face and tell you he loves you.

4. Someone who makes you feel like the most beautiful woman in the room, regardless of how many gorgeous women are there.
5. The feeling of being completely understood without the uncertainty of how long the feeling will last.

Instead of longing for these traits, qualities, and experiences in your past, place them ahead of you in your future. Embrace the idea that they're still out there for you. That you can and will once again experience all the beauty of your last relationship, only without the pain, anguish, disappointment, confusion, compromise, and despair of the past. You and you alone create your future. Why not paint a more exciting and vibrant picture?

Starting today, stop looking backward and just walk away instead. Slowly but surely move fearlessly into the future. Whether you know it or not, your future is shifting into a more fantastic and feel-good shape as you read this chapter. It's up to you to continue the reinvention process. Go ahead, Girl. Get busy!

Pitfall #3: You're so Afraid of Getting Hurt Again That You Shut Down

Even after you walk away from the wrong relationship and start moving into your future, there are still plenty of pitfalls to watch out for. One of the most common ones is falling into the unhealthy belief system that relationships are so painful, disappointing, and dramatic that you never want to try again. Convinced that love really is a battlefield, you wear bullet-proof armor, emerging from your post-breakup cocoon like a wounded warrior. And while learning lessons from past relationships is important, you haven't become any wiser. You've just become emotionally unavailable and psychologically wounded.

Results include the following:

- Any time a guy shows the slightest bit of interest in you, you become increasingly suspicious and find a multitude of reasons to blow him off, ditch him, or dump him.
- Whenever you meet a cute guy who could have potential, you instantly become critical of everything about him, ensuring that there's no possible way he's dating material.
- Any time your single friends experience dating success with a great guy, you find reasons why they're the exception to the rule that there are no other good men left.
- You fill your free time with busy work, rarely (if ever) accepting invitations to social activities outside your comfort zone.

Sound familiar?

Let me be clear about one thing. When you're in the process of healing your heart, it's important to honor your need to protect yourself. You should never put yourself out there before you're ready. But the post-relationship rut I'm talking about happens long *after* you've healed your heart. When you're no longer picking up the pieces of your old life, but are so fearful of creating a new life that you opt to stay in limbo indefinitely, avoiding the dating scene, rejecting any guy who comes within 50 feet of you, and in general constructing emotional walls that are so high no one can climb over them.

By choosing to stay stuck in this scenario, you think you're playing it safe and ensuring no one can ever hurt your heart again. You may be right. But you're also missing out on life and the amazing possibilities that await you. By taking yourself out of the game before things have a chance to get interesting, you basically tell the universe to remove you from the running for a fantastic future, and potentially miss out on incredible adventures, including:

- Rediscovering how amazing you really are, and what life has to offer you once you shed your post-breakup cocoon and learn to fly.
- Applying lessons learned, becoming emotionally healthier, and eventually making better choices when it comes to the type of men you attract.
- The opportunity to become an object of desire, with multitudes of men calling to ask *you* out.
- The chance to re-create what's possible for you in your life, career, romance, family, health, and spirituality.
- The gift of falling in love again, this time with someone truly amazing who will love you back with all he's got.

Do you really want to miss out on all that? Life's too short to stop trying. Instead of permanently benching yourself and your chances of recreating your happily-ever-after future, why not instead apply those hard-learned lessons and honor your healing heart by holding yourself accountable and making better choices moving forward? There's a whole lot more in store for you, but you have to be willing to take the risk. You also have to be ready to make mistakes, possibly skin your knees along the way, and always be willing to pick yourself up, dust yourself off, and try again. Scary? Sure. But oh-so-worth it!

Pitfall #4: You Repeat the Same Dating and Relationship Patterns

When you look back at your relationship history, do you see a familiar (and possibly dysfunctional) pattern? The answer may be yes if you find yourself in relationship after relationship with seemingly different types of men, only to discover the same lackluster and unfulfilling results, including:

- Dating yet another man who puts you down, doesn't believe in you, and constantly criticizes you.
- Attracting another workaholic or addict who puts his addictions and demons before you.
- Finding yet another man who has intimacy issues and can't open himself up to a real and lasting connection.
- Falling for another man who's not your equal, just because he's the only one pursuing you.
- Feeling frustrated that you just can't make a relationship work—again!

Most women get stuck in this rut until they make the conscious choice to wise up and change their behavior. And yes, changing the kind of results you experience starts with Y-O-U and your behavior. After all, you're the one saying yes to the workaholics, addicts, commitmentphobes, and other emotionally stunted men. You're the one agreeing to continue seeing them even though you know they're not your equal or you don't like the way they're treating you. Until you're willing to say no to Mr. Wrong (even when you have no idea when Mr. Right will show up), you're going to get the exact same results you've always gotten.

Starting today, you need to believe that better dating results are possible for you. This may take some practice, but begin with this very simple exercise. Ask yourself how you define dating, relationships, and/or love. Start by saying, "Dating is . . ." and fill in the blank. If your answers include words like hopeless, frustrating, lame, stressful, disappointing, and so on, do you see how you're actually manifesting those results based on your belief system?

Now, redefine dating, relationships, and/or love by saying "Dating/Relationships/Love is . . ." and creating a brand new healthy and happy vocabulary. Words you can incorporate may include happy, healthy, exciting, abundant, available, fun, freeing, mutual, and so on. The goal here is to get you out of your dating rut by reinvigorating how you feel about your chances of experiencing the kind of relationship you want and deserve.

1. Review the pitfalls you may be stuck in. Which resonate most? Starting today, how can you extricate yourself from it? Make an action plan and stick to it.

2. If needed, re-create your dating vocabulary by making a list of how you used to view love and relationships, then replace any old, negative, limiting definitions with happy and healthy words. Practice this exercise aloud morning and night for thirty days.

chapter 6

the million-dollar question

Before you can successfully leave the past behind and make room for Mr. Next and Mr. Right, you've got to get a crystal-clear idea of what's next for you, not just in love but in life. How do you get clear? By asking yourself this simple question: *How do you want to be loved?*

Re-read the question a couple of times to yourself. Maybe even ask yourself the question out loud.

As you ask yourself this question, what feelings, thoughts, and emotions arise? Do you feel uncertain, anxious, excited, fearful, inspired, or any combination of those emotions? Regardless of what comes up, it's important to honor the feelings. It's also essential to start answering the question. Whether you know it or not, your brilliant future already exists. The details may be fuzzy, but it's out there waiting for you. Your job today and as you continue moving forward is to clarify that future by answering the question.

So ask yourself again: *How do you want to be loved?*

What is your initial response to that question? Is it:

A. *I have no idea.*
B. *I just want to be loved. Why do I have to define it beyond that?*
C. *I want to be loved the way INSERT YOUR EX'S NAME used to love me. It wasn't perfect, but it was pretty good.*
D. *I want to be loved like I've never been loved before. The love that comes to me is effortless, passionate, beautiful, transformative, freeing, blissful, equal, available, exquisite. . . .*

Which of those responses resonate most with you? Keep in mind there are no right or wrong answers here. However, the way you answer the question affects the kind of future that's unfolding.

Let me clarify that. How you answer the question is how love will show up for you in *all* areas of your life. So if you answered A. *I have no idea*, what kind of results do you think you'll manifest? More to the point, do you think love will show up at all? Given that you have no idea what it will look or feel like, what if it shows up and you don't recognize it? What a shame!

If you answered B. *I just want to be loved. Why do I have to define it beyond that?*, how do you think love will show up for you? More than likely, you'll let love come to you in many different forms. You'll say yes to men who are wildly inappropriate because at least they asked, you'll take jobs just because they were offered, apartments because they were available, and friends because they happened to come into your life. Along the way, you'll often wonder why life and love seem so random, and why amazing things happen to other people while your life just seems like one long series of coincidences. While this is better than no results, it's not exactly core-shaking or pulse-quickening.

If your answer leaned toward C. *I want to be loved the way INSERT YOUR EX'S NAME used to love me. It wasn't perfect, but it was pretty good*, you will most likely experience moderate levels of happiness and satisfaction when it comes to life and love. But truthfully, with a belief system that basically says, "Well, I've never had much success with love, so I guess I never will," or "That fairytale kind of love doesn't exist so I have to settle for whatever I can get," all you're really doing is repeating the same limiting beliefs over and over and over. And not just in the romantic love department—in every area of your life. With limited thinking capping what's possible for you, you will most likely enjoy a mediocre life with mediocre results.

- You'll get your annual cost-of-living increase at your job, but never that awesome promotion you secretly dream about (let alone take a leap into your passion profession).
- You'll sit by and watch while all of your friends marry, settle down, and have children, and actually convince yourself that you're not worthy even though you secretly desire everything they have.
- You'll live within your means, but will never experience true abundance (translation: You never take that splurge-tastic Mediterranean cruise you've always wanted to, or trade your paid-off SUV for the Prius you know is more aligned with your core values because you'd have to make car payments for a little while, or buy your first home because it feels like too much of a financial stretch, and so on).
- You'll continue to occasionally date guys who ask you out, and forever wonder why the men who are interested in you

are not your equals while the men you're interested in can't be bothered to give you the time of day.

- From time to time, you'll ask yourself if this is as good as it gets, but, more often than not, you'll accept this so-so life because wanting more is too uncomfortable and uncertain. You're not a risk-taker so it's better to stay put.

When you look at these lives and choices, do they sound eerily familiar? Is it like glimpsing your future? And if so, how does it feel? Is there a certain level of resigned acceptance or did that vision of the future scare the crap out of you?

Again, there are no right or wrong answers to the question. However, I'm hoping that you're waking up to the idea that *if* anything and everything is possible (and it is), you can become a gutsy girl and go for it.

Now, if you answered D. *I want to be loved like I've never been loved before. The love that comes to me is effortless, passionate, beautiful, transformative, freeing, blissful, equal, available, exquisite . . .* you're already a gutsy girl. So what do you think will happen for you?

You'll begin to shift your life experiences in profound and effortless ways. Dating opportunities will present themselves around every corner. Love will come to you more easily. Career opportunities will effortlessly appear before you. Life challenges will be easily resolved with little to no drama. All because you said yes to the possibility that even though you'd never before experienced real and lasting love, you were open to the idea that it was available to you. Amen to that!

If the question scares or intimidates you, honor those feelings. But don't skip over this chapter or ignore the question. You've come this far. Why not continue being brave and bold by summoning your inner strength, digging deep, and searching for exciting answers? Even if you've never experienced such beautiful abundance and possibility before, for just a moment, humor yourself and dream B-I-G.

Let's say you can design the most perfect love possible. This is not limited to romantic love. This is how love will show up for you in friendships, career, financial abundance, health, and spirituality. What does limitless love look like to you?

If you're stumped for answers, try this definition on for size:

Love is an unlimited resource that effortlessly flows into my life, fills me up, brings joy to myself and everyone around me, energizes my soul, feeds my mind, leaves me with a sense of peace, heals all wounds, is abundantly available, and rocks my world.

Better yet, write your very own magical and transformative answer to the question now.

How do I want to be loved? (Remember, dream big!)

_____

_____

_____

_____

Once you're done with this exercise, read it back. Repeat it out loud.

How does it feel to define what's possible for you in those abundant terms? Regardless of what your childhood was like, how unsatisfying love and relationships have been for you in the past, and how you feel about your life in this very moment, do you see how your belief system can powerfully shift just from opening your mind to the idea of what's possible for you?

If you're willing to take a leap and answer the question *How do I want to be loved?* in ways you never before thought possible, what might your future look like? How could it and would it look different from what you thought it would look like just five minutes ago?

Facebook Friends Weigh In

When I asked the question *How do you want to be loved?* on Facebook, here's what some of my fab friends said. . . .

"Love yourself—then you'll always have someone to love and be loved by." —REVVELL

"Love others the way you want to be loved. What comes around goes around." —GIL

"Learning to love and accept yourself as the unique individual you are helps others know how to love and accept you. It all starts from within." —KARLA

By shifting your belief system and dreaming big when answering the question *How do I want to be loved?* your future begins to take on exciting new possibilities. These possibilities may include:

1. A new job opportunity suddenly landing in your lap.
2. That cutie you've been eyeing at the gym finally asking you out.
3. The condo you were crazy about falling out of escrow, inviting you to make an offer.
4. A financial windfall coming your way out of the blue.
5. Your painting/script/monologue getting accepted into the big exhibit/contest/show.

Are you starting to get the picture? By answering that simple yet profound question, you are actually re-creating the future that will unfold before you. Talk about powerful!

Back to the Future

To get a better understanding of how your future shapes your present, try to do the following exercise. It's a powerful and profound guide that will further illustrate to you the power of redefining how you want to be loved. To get started, read this next section in its entirety, and then do the exercise on your own. If you'd like guidance, an audio version of this exercise is available for free by going to *www.IfHesNottheOneWhoIs* *.com/bonusaudio*.

First, get comfortable, preferably in a comfy chair, lying on a couch, or in bed. Close your eyes and take a few deep, cleansing breaths. Let any racing thoughts that clutter your mind slowly fall away. Once your mind has slowed, take a few more deep breaths, center yourself, and ease into a more relaxed state.

Next, imagine in your mind's eye that there are five closed doorways in front of you. These five doorways represent the various paths you can take into your future. Here's what each doorway represents. . . .

Doorway Number One: The door on the far left is the doorway to the worst possible future you can imagine. Death, pain, loss, anger, and betrayal lie ahead through doorway number one. You can even see, smell, and sense smoke, heat, and decay through the closed door. What lies ahead in that future is nothing but misery, despair, and loss.

Doorway Number Two: Next to door number one is door number two. Behind this door is the faint odor of burnt toast, decaying trash, and general unpleasantness. While it's not as dark, sinister, or scary as doorway number one, you know that doorway number two offers a similarly bleak forecast of the future. Get a sense for how you feel about the future behind this door before moving on to the next.

Doorway Number Three: By comparison to the first two doors, doorway number three doesn't look or seem so bad. Through it, there is a moderately mediocre future. Nothing to get excited about, but nothing terribly tragic either. You could easily navigate the life behind this door but know that there would never be great love, abundance, or possibility.

Doorway Number Four: Next, doorway number four holds the path to an okay future. Again, not bleak or brutal, but nothing exceptionally beautiful or breathtaking either. Life would be all right if you walked through this doorway into the future. But is a so-so existence what you truly want and desire?

Doorway Number Five: And then there's doorway number five. Through this magnificent doorway, you can sense warmth, love, abundant energy, and even the faint smell of warm chocolate chip cookies. Doorway number five leads to the awesome future. A future full of possibility, pleasure, joy, abundance, and so much more.

With your eyes still closed, picture all five closed doors once more. Really get a sense for what's behind each closed door. Ask yourself which door you want to open and step through. Which future sounds most appealing and possible to you? Without any judgment, pick your door. Once you've chosen your door, imagine yourself walking toward that particular door. And as you get closer, the door opens, showing you a glimpse of what's inside. Pay attention to the sights, smells, and sounds before you. Take a deep breath here, and then when you're ready, imagine yourself walking through the door and into your future.

As you step into the future, what do you see? Look around you. Are you inside or outside? There is a woman in front of you. It's your future self. Take a good look at her. What does she look like? How old does she seem? Observe as much detail as possible that will tell you how far into the future you have traveled. A few months, a few years, or many years into the future? How does your future self look? Is she happy, sad, stressed, or peaceful? Take a long look at her.

Next, expand your awareness to see that there is a man with your future self. He's the man you have manifested into your future. What does he look like? How is he interacting with your future self? Are they happy and laughing or sad and serious? Watch as they embrace. See the love that exists between them. Is it warm and tender or tight and tense?

Move closer now. Feel the energy between your future self and this man. How does it feel to be loved by him? Record as many sensory experiences as possible, including any of the following that come up for you:

1. Imagine his arms around you, holding you close. What does that feel like?
2. Imagine him nuzzling his nose to your hair, whispering in your ear. What does he say?
3. Imagine him kissing you passionately on the lips. How does it make you feel?
4. Picture the two of you doing an activity together. What are you doing and how does it make you feel?
5. Imagine that it's the end of the day. Does he kiss you good-bye and walk out the door or does he take your hand and lead you upstairs?

Experience this future for a few more moments. Take in any last remaining sensory stimulation, including sights, sounds, smells, touches, tastes. Also take note of whether there are other people in that future and who they are. Are they familiar or strangers? Grown-ups or children?

When you're ready, inhale deeply, and as you exhale, take a mental snapshot of the future you just experienced. Then, take a step back, move back through the doorway you chose, and return to the present. Take a few slow deep breaths, wiggle your hands and feet back to room awareness, and open your eyes.

Spend a few minutes writing down every detail you experienced in your future. Start by writing down which doorway you chose and why. Again, there's no judgment here. Next, describe your future self. What did she look like, how far into the future was this, and what was she doing? Next, share everything you remember about the man in your future. What did he look like, how did he sound, and what did it feel like to be loved by him? Finally, record any other details about the people, place, and activities going on around you in the future you just visited.

After you've recorded everything you experienced and saw, be sure to capture how you felt physically during this exercise as well as how you're feeling right now. During the exercise, did your body become tingly, lighter, and more relaxed? Or did it tense up and become tight? Some people report a sense of lightness that comes over them during this exercise. Don't worry if it didn't happen for you. Everyone's experience is different. Simply record as much information as you possibly can. Then re-read everything.

How vivid did your trip into the future become for you? And how do you feel about getting to that future now that you're back in the present? If the future was beautiful and blissful, you're most likely excited to take steps toward it, starting right now. Or, if the future wasn't so bright, you may want to make some changes and adjustments to your current life and present circumstances to alter what's next for you.

In doing this exercise, you begin to connect the dots between where you are today and where you think you're going. Once you understand that how you feel about your future affects every decision you make today, tomorrow, and so on, you can start embracing a happier and healthier outlook about your future.

───────── ***Real Futures Revealed*** ─────────

When we've done this exercise together, here's what some of my clients reported seeing in their fab futures. . . .

"I saw myself in cowboy boots. I've never worn cowboy boots in my life! But boy, was I happy!"—Shauna

"I was with this amazing man and we were in our pajamas, enjoying our morning coffee in bed. There was a little girl in the bed with us, snuggling, and I was pregnant. We all looked so content."—Stephanie

"I don't know exactly where I was, somewhere in the woods in this beautiful cabin overlooking a river. I was cooking for my man. We were laughing, having a great time. And I don't cook!"—Gene

"I saw my ex and two little children. I don't want my ex *or* more children, especially not with him. Something has to change. I have to change."—Luisa

"I was in my house surrounded by the people I love most. My friends, family, we were all celebrating some big occasion. And there he was, this gorgeous man from my future. Just standing back, smiling at me, loving me. It felt amazing."—Kira

The more you can connect to your future, the clearer you'll be about where you're going and what needs to happen next. If there are areas in your future that you want to shift and change, know that it's possible. In fact, it's totally in your power to change anything and everything! Plus, by connecting to your future, getting excited about where you're going, and getting clear about what's next for you, you begin to easily and effortlessly call in Mr. Next. When he shows up, you're better able to recognize him, not to mention relax and have fun with him because you know that if it turns out he's not the fabulous man in your future (AKA Mr. Right), another guy will come along soon enough and take his place. After all, there *is* a groovy guy out there waiting for you. And if one guy gets away, another will come along soon enough. (Didn't see a man in your visit to the future and wish you had? It's not too late to manifest him. Simply repeat the exercise over the next few weeks until you magically and masterfully call in your perfect partner. Remember, practice makes perfect!)

Loving Y-O-U

At the beginning of this chapter, I told you that there is no one-size-fits-all vision of happily ever after, and it's true. Everyone's vision of that future will be different, based on their own wants and needs. But here's what's the same in every picture: When you answer the question *How do I want to be loved?*, you ultimately redefine how you will love yourself. That's where it all starts—with self-love. By learning to treat yourself with kindness, compassion, respect, and self-care, you in turn show others how to treat you. However, if you choose to remain in lack, doubt, insecurity, uncertainty, and despair, people will pick up on that, too. It will affect how they interact with you. And it will ultimately affect the kinds of people who are drawn to you.

By learning to love and honor yourself with or without a man, on good days and bad, and regardless of how much money is in the bank, how you performed at work that day, or if you said or did all the right things, you show the world (and everyone in it) just how much you value the most important person in your life—Y-O-U. In turn, you make it that much easier for others to treat you with kindness, compassion, respect, and love.

So if it all starts with you, what will you do differently, starting today? How will you treat yourself better? What behaviors, beliefs, and habits need to shift? How can you better celebrate your fabulous self starting right this very minute? Here are some ideas:

1. When those hypercritical, judgmental, and demeaning thoughts pop into your head, pause for a minute. Listen to them. And then reframe them into something more positive and loving. For example, *I'm so fat today!* can shift into *I love myself no matter what.* This may be challenging at first, but keep practicing.
2. When you cross paths with a cute guy, instead of running the other way or averting your gaze like you're used to doing, stop, make eye contact, and smile. If he's got half a brain, he'll pick up your cue and start a conversation. If not, no worries. He wasn't worth your time. Next!
3. Have a bad day? Instead of parking it on the couch, mindlessly watching TV and stuffing your face with comfort food until you feel sick (and worse than you already do), treat yourself to a few bites of chocolate while reclining in a nurturing bubble bath, complete with relaxing music, and hot tea or red wine. This way, you get the comfort food and relaxation without the guilt!

4. Screw up at work? Instead of spending the next week convinced you'll be fired, be proactive. Confidently approach your boss, own up to your mistakes, and chalk it up to lessons learned. You don't need to beat yourself up to wise up.
5. The next time a crush blows you off, instead of internalizing it and blaming yourself for doing something wrong, remind yourself that you are fabulous. If he can't handle you? Too bad! Life's too short to get hung up on Mr. Wrong.

1. Take some time to answer the question *How do I want to be loved?* Give yourself permission to be brave and bold in your response!

2. Do the exercise where you choose a doorway and visit your future. For audio guidance, go to *www.LisaSteadman.com/visitmyfuture.* When you're done with the exercise, record as much detail of that future as possible. Ask yourself this: How did that exercise affect my feelings about the future? What will I do differently from now on to ensure a better future? Repeat this exercise as needed in the coming weeks.

3. How can you better celebrate your fabulous self starting right this very minute? Come up with at least five ways to start loving and nurturing yourself. Have fun with this exercise!

chapter 7

keeping up with ms. and mrs. jones

Be honest. Fairytales and future visions aren't the only thing f***ing with your head these days, are they? Society—not to mention biology—may not feel like your friend right about now. From the incessant *tick, tick, tick* of your biological clock to the barrage of media messages telling you that time may be running out on your search for Mr. Right (not to mention your chance to have babies), it's no wonder you sometimes feel like you're hyperventilating. And then there are other women. You know who I'm talking about. Those ridiculously over-achieving, size two jeans–wearing, luxury car–driving, bling-tastic diamond ring–sporting, perfectly coifed and manicured, baby-toting babes who effortlessly have it all. Well, them and all those other regular-sized girls who somehow managed to pull ahead when you weren't looking and are dominating the love and baby race, even though they have cellulite, debt, and bad skin.

If you're really honest, it's these regular women who make you feel the worst about yourself. What do they have that you don't? And how did they snag their dream guy while you're still going on first dates with men who hold the dinner candle up to your face to check out your wrinkles (a true story from the trenches!), whose definition of monogamy depends on what they've been caught doing, and who may still live at home with their parents?

In the new millennium, it's not men who have you feeling inadequate about your single status. It's women. And not just other women. You're just as guilty. Whether consciously or unconsciously, you may be perpetuating social norms and the belief that there's something inherently wrong with a single woman without children who's past a certain age.

So what's a girl to do? It's time to shed some light on this estrogen-fueled epidemic in hopes of healing your own insecurities as well as turning down the volume on your collective need to keep up with the Ms. and Mrs. Joneses of the world. Let's get to work!

Meet Mrs. Jones

First, let's talk about those seemingly perfect women who just by living and breathing make you feel absolutely awful about yourself. These are the girls who married in their twenties, had their first baby by thirty, sport a rock the size of a marble on their left ring finger, whose husbands have six-figure-and-up incomes, and not only do these women *not* have to work, but they don't even have stretch marks from the 2.5 kids they've given birth to.

I don't have to guess at what five letter word you just uttered (or shouted). I've felt the same way a time or two. But why? These women are not to be feared. And believe it or not, they're not on the planet just to make you feel bad about yourself. The truth is, you have no idea what their life is actually like. Are they happy? Do they have a blissful relationship with their husband? Is motherhood everything it's cracked up to be? Do they miss having a career?

These are important questions to ask whenever your disdain (or fully engaged rage) surfaces as you try to maneuver around them and their designer baby stroller on the bike path, while impatiently waiting your turn at the deli counter, or when trying to talk over their screaming baby while catching up with a fellow single gal pal at brunch.

You shouldn't be expected to feel sorry for these women who effortlessly have everything that may still be on your wish list. But you want to take a more compassionate approach to them. Instead of subscribing to the belief that these women purposely have it all just to chip away at your self-esteem, why not take a step back and realize that their path has its own unique set of challenges? And while life in the wife and motherhood lane definitely has its perks, it also has its challenges. Even the happiest of these ladies who lunch occasionally wonder about the road less traveled. They wonder if they married too young, had children too soon, if they could have or should have stayed single longer and held out for a more suitable candidate. And while they may never openly admit that they envy your savvy single lifestyle, believe it or not, they do.

- They admire your ability to financially provide for yourself without a man.
- They envy the fast track your career seems to be on.
- That solo trip you took to Europe? They can only dream of exploring foreign countries without a crying baby, cranky toddler, and/or overbearing in-laws.

- While you get to sleep as late as you like on weekends, the idea of sleeping in on a Saturday is nothing more than a pipe dream to them.

Do you see how the fabulous life you've been coveting comes with its own set of compromises and headaches? The truth is, these women who seemingly have it all are not to be feared or hated. It's time to understand that their life path is just another version of your own.

So why do you have to be the one to feel empathy for them rather than the other way around? Because you're smart, savvy, and successful. Because you have the luxury of time, sleep, and personal space. And because if these women ever got a quiet moment to themselves, I'm sure they'd practice empathy for you and your challenges. They may not know your challenges, worries, and fears—but only because they're preoccupied with their own. Mrs. Jones is not the enemy. And neither are you. We're all just women trying to make the best of our lives based on our life choices.

And Now for Ms. Jones. . . .

Take another look around. How many amazing, successful, savvy single or on-the-road-to-matrimony women do you know? Between work, networking, friends, and family, probably quite a few, right?

Now, be honest. When something good happens to one of these single women, how do you respond? With a joy-filled "Woohoo!" or with a snarling and insincere "Good for you." Remember, I said be honest.

Let's try that again. When good fortune smiles upon a single-and-ready-to-mingle female coworker, neighbor, or friend, do you:

1. Genuinely experience joy on her behalf, inspired by whatever she's manifested, and use it as energy to manifest good in your life?
2. Experience a mix of happiness and envy, hopeful but uncertain that something good may come your way next?
3. Immediately feel a sense of injustice, wondering why amazing things happen to others but never to you?

If you chose #1, were you totally transparent or wishfully thinking? If your answer was genuine, congratulations! You have a healthy and happy attitude toward your fellow females. If your answer leaned toward option #2 or #3, don't feel bad. Society has pretty much programmed women to fervently compete with one another, engaging in all out warfare until one fierce female remains standing, victorious, with a red rose in her hand and a bachelor on her arm.

Think about all those magazine covers you scan while in the line at the grocery store. It's been years since Jennifer Aniston divorced Brad Pitt, but the rivalry between Brangelina and Jen (and now even between Brad and Angie) lives on weekly in scathing headlines. And look at how the media portrays female friendship (think *The Hills*'s Audrina Patridge and Kristin Cavallari, or Paris Hilton and Nicole Richie). If we believed what television, magazines, and the media tell us, we'd think that women can't genuinely be friends with one another and instead, we should surround ourselves with frenemies.

It's okay to feel whatever you honestly feel when good things happen to the women in your life. By clearly identifying the feelings that come up for you (both good and bad), you're better able to see how you may be sabotaging your own success and happiness by squelching others' triumphs.

If you struggle to feel happy for your female friends when good things happen to them, you most likely subscribe to a scarcity belief about what's possible for you. You may also believe that there's a limit to the amount of love, success, happiness, and abundance that's available in the world. And if some other woman snags a second date with a real cutie, buys the car of her dreams, wins $50,000 playing the lotto, or magically lands a fab new job, it feels like something's being taken away from you. It's like there's one less opportunity coming your way.

Do you see how limiting that is? If the law of attraction is real (and thankfully it is!), by living in lack, subscribing to scarcity fears, and experiencing overwhelming envy toward others, you don't leave any room in your life for your own good fortune. But before you write yourself off as a hopeless cause doomed to end up alone and miserable while others get everything their hearts desire, keep reading. Time has *not* run out on your chance to get it right. It's just time to shift your thinking.

And don't think you're alone in your feelings of lack, uncertainty, and scarcity. Collectively, as women we've seemingly lost our way. Once upon a time, we were communal, nurturing, and loyal to our tribe. Now more than ever we're competitive, combative, and downright nasty. Our sisterhood is struggling. While we may never be able to identify exactly when it became more acceptable to tear each other down than lift each other up, it's time to turn down the narcissistic desire to rip our fellow females to emotional shreds.

Now's the time to put an end to our *winner take all* approach to other women. Here's how. Starting today, embody your most supportive and nurturing self. When a woman you know scores a promotion, buys her first home, gets engaged, or reaches her goal weight, instead of tearing her down behind her back, celebrate her success as if it were your own. Truthfully, success is a collaborative process. No man, and especially no woman, is an island. So instead of acting out of scarcity, hoarding the good that comes your way, and begrudging the blessings that go to others, treat each and every success as if it were collective and communal. You may be surprised at how happiness, joy, fortune, and opportunity exponentially grow when given the chance. Instead of trying to elbow your way past your fellow Ms. and Mrs. Joneses, extend your hand, clasp fingers, and cross the finish line together.

This may take some time to fully embrace, especially if you've been secretly seething about other women's success for years. And that's okay. Like anything else in life, your new belief system is going to take some practice. Start by creating at least one new belief around other people's success. It may sound something like this:

The success of others leads to my own success and happiness.

I am inspired by the good that happens to others.

When another woman succeeds, it lifts me up.

I humbly and graciously celebrate the success of my sisters.

When one of us succeeds, we all succeed!

Once you've chosen the new belief(s) that works for you, practice it every day for thirty days. Write it in your journal. Say it out loud. Look yourself in the eye in the mirror and repeat it daily. Meditate on it. Pray about it. Do whatever practice works for you so that you fully embrace the celebration of sisterhood. Whether you know it or not, this will dramatically shift your relationships with both women *and* men. By not coming from a place of lack or competition, your energy will become lighter and more attractive. You'll not only start manifesting stronger bonds with amazing and supportive women, but you'll begin to call in far more fabulous men than you ever imagined possible. Talk about a win-win!

Here's another incentive to cut these women who seem to effortlessly have it all some slack. Hating/being crazy jealous of them is actually killing your chances of snagging and bagging your very own dream man. How? Believe it or not, men *are* perceptive. They pay attention to the women in their life. If and when you're huffing and puffing about how unfair it is that the Mrs. and Ms. Jones of the world have it all while you're slogging away in a Corporate America cubicle, and your only social excitement during the week is your nightly date with Jon Stewart, men see your frustration, angst, and impatience. They can sense it in your negative energy. They can hear it in your snide comments about other women. And they can see it when you force that fake smile upon being introduced to one of these females you consider a frenemy.

Whether you know it or not, men are on to you. So do yourself and your dating future a huge favor and relinquish your need to secretly plot these ladies' demise. Instead of wasting any more of your fabulous time wishing bad karma could and would smack the Mrs. and Ms. Joneses of the world upside their perfectly coiffed heads, stop. Take a step back. Embrace the fact that you'll be much more likely to attract great guys if you feel good about yourself and your life. And that starts with putting a stop to your death wish for your fellow females. Learn it, love it, live it!

The Curse of "The Tick"

Now that you've turned down the volume on your competitive streak with other women, it's time to dial into another massive saboteur that may be keeping you from loving your life right now. Without the need to compete with your fellow females, there may be someone (or something) else you're feeling the need to beat.

Meet your biological clock.

Do you fear that time's running out on your chance to win the baby race? Are your friends married, having children, and asking you when it's your turn? Or worse, is your mother dropping hints about how much she's just dying to be a grandmother? Or, when it comes to the baby race, are you your own worst enemy, beating yourself up for allegedly falling too far behind?

Consciously or unconsciously, you may be receiving some seriously sabotaging messages from society and your loved ones, not to mention those demeaning conversations you have in your head with yourself. You know the ones. They go something like this:

With my thick thighs/thinning hair/student loan debt/ crooked teeth, no man will ever want to marry me!

At this point, I'll be lucky to have just one baby.

By the time I finally get it right and get married, my eggs will be ancient history.

There's no point in even trying anymore. I'm going to end up alone, miserable, and childless.

Sound familiar? The messages we tell ourselves and the messages we subconsciously pick up from society can be brutal. And while we can't completely cut out the crap, we can fashion a better filter, one that turns down the volume on your panic, and has a more realistic approach to your personal timeline.

Instead of feeling left behind by your friends and all the other women in the world who marry, procreate, and nest in their twenties and early thirties, cut yourself some slack. Your timeline may be different, but it's no less valid or exciting. By *not* settling down and becoming a mom during those formative baby-making years, you get to climb the corporate ladder, make your own money, buy your own property, date a variety of interesting and available guys, and redefine what happily ever after looks like for you, complete with the memories of going topless on your solo European vacation, skydiving while strapped to a super cute instructor, and being the most sought after single at speed dating. (Or whatever other exhilarating memories you wish to create for yourself during your savvy single years.)

But what if what I really want is to have a baby? you may be asking right about now. *What if marriage, motherhood, and minivans are part of the package I thought I signed up for?*

There's still time for you. But first, you may need to take a chill pill. While your biological clock is real (and totally explains those emotional surges you feel when you see a newborn baby or a handsome man toting an adorable toddler), it doesn't have to be your worst enemy. Yes, there are optimal child-bearing years in a woman's life, and your chances of conception gradually and then dramatically drop as you get older. But guess what? You don't have to be thirty-five and fertile to have a baby these days. The miracles of modern medicine make motherhood possible for women of all ages, whether they conceive naturally or through the help of a fertility specialist. Plus, adoption and surrogacy are fantastic options should you find that by the time you're ready to settle down and start a family you're not physically capable of getting pregnant. It's not a judgment on who you are as a woman. It's a fact of life in our modern world that people are waiting a whole lot longer to marry and start families. So rather than beat yourself up for being behind schedule or at the back of the pack in the baby race, slow down, calm down, and reassess your personal life path. You're not ridiculously late for your happily ever after. You're right on time.

1. Are there women in your life toward whom you've been secretly harboring envy, anger, jealousy, and feelings of injustice? Make a list and then ask yourself how you can turn down the volume on your negative emotions and instead celebrate their life choices and success.

2. What negative messages are you picking up on or sending yourself about where you are on the journey toward happily ever after? Write them down. Review them. Work to reframe into healthier beliefs and release the negative ones.

3. If you're hearing your biological clock tick, can you turn down the volume and embrace the idea that you're not behind schedule for your dream life? Instead, open your mind to the new knowledge that it's never too late to marry, have children, or live your dream life. But in order to get there, you've got to release the pressure you put on yourself and embrace your savvy single life.

chapter 8

an ex marks the plot

On the journey away from your past and into your new and improved future, there are many checkpoints. When you stop at these checkpoints, it's important to assess and celebrate how far you've come as well as where you're going next. Along the way, you'll meet plenty of Mr. Nexts, apply lessons learned, and, if all goes well, you'll eventually manifest Mr. Right. But before you can cross those items off your list, there's an important checkpoint to pass. And it has to do with your ex. Specifically, it has to do with whether or not you're over your ex.

Before you roll your eyes at me, stop. While it's true that you may no longer be lurking on his Facebook and Twitter pages (or are you?), that his memory has been 100 percent deleted from your online and offline life (right?), and long gone are the days where even the mere mention of his name had you reaching for a box of tissues and the Ben & Jerry's, it's still possible that you may somehow still be hung up on what's his name.

So let me ask you a question. Are you over your ex?

On a conscious level, the answer is most likely yes. But what about on an unconscious level? How *might* you unknowingly be sabotaging your efforts to meet Mr. Next by being far too focused on Mr. Ex? What follows are some signs you may not have fully exorcised the ex from your head and heart. See if any of them feel frighteningly familiar.

- If you still catch yourself starting sentences with, "My boy-friend—I mean my *ex*-boyfriend says/does/thinks . . . ."
- Every time you're on a date, you look at the person across from you and think "This guy can't even compare to INSERT YOUR EX'S NAME."
- Even after all this time, you're still beating yourself up for how the relationship ended and what you could have done differently to save it. (Suffering from a serious case of the *If only I'd's* . . . .)
- Whenever anything goes wrong in your life, you get mad at your ex and/or hear his demeaning words ringing in your ears ("I told you you were weak/pathetic/needy!" "I knew you couldn't make it on your own two feet!")

If you find yourself falling prey to one or more of the above scenarios on a regular basis, now's the time to put some tough love into practice so that you can kick that bad habit and ultimately evict your ex from your healed heart. He doesn't belong there anymore. And until he gets the heave ho, there's just no room for Mr. Next, let alone Mr. Right. Starting today, it's time to emotionally kick your ex to the curb once and for all. Here's how.

Leggo Your Neggo

If you blame your ex for every rotten, lousy, horrible thing that's happened to you since the breakup (if and when your car breaks down, you lose your job, your dog runs away), you're not over him.

Now, if your breakup was particularly tough, there will most likely be times when you actually feel like your ex ruined your life. That's normal. What's not normal or healthy is to buy into the belief system that your entire future is screwed, courtesy of your ex. While you cannot change the past or any of the repercussions you've experienced because of your ex, you have the opportunity to actively choose how you want to handle these minor and major setbacks. After all, the past is the past. You can't wave a magic wand and do it over again, but you *can* alter the course of your fab future.

from the *fearless female files* . . .

"Every time something bad happens I go right back down to the pity party of 'Look what he's done to me.' That does not help me one bit. I need to look at it as one more step to having him totally out of my life and on to a better and happier time. I think if I can start looking at the good in all that happens, I won't be so angry with him anymore."—linda

See, up until now you may have believed that your ex controlled what came next for you. But guess what? *You're* the only one in charge of your future. *You* decide how to handle challenges, setbacks, and disappointment. Most of them would be there with or without your ex. And yes, there may be some ex-specific setbacks (for example, if his bad credit somehow mars your financial status, if you had to give up your animals because you owned them together, if you had to shell out major cash to move while he got to stay put, and so on). Again, you choose how you deal with these things, and you can handle them like the grown up woman you are, or you can handle them like a victim. *Look how screwed up he made me!* should so *not* be your new anthem. Playing the victim is neither sexy nor smart. It's actually beneath you and a total waste of your time.

Right here and now, honor your healed heart and dump your need to blame and shame your ex. It's not necessary. And it only keeps you stuck in the pain of the past while your ex is long gone. To celebrate your progress and accelerate your future, let go and move on.

Pedestal Pusher

Brutal honesty time. If and when you meet a new guy, do you constantly compare him to your ex? And if so, does he ever measure up? Whether it's a conscious or unconscious choice, you may have become blind to your ex's bad qualities, completely magnifying his good ones until you can no longer see straight. To help you regain 20/20 vision, here are some sure-fire signs that your ex is still holding court in your heart:

- When you think about your ex, memories of the good times and his good qualities flood back without any reminders of his negative traits and the bad times.
- After a string of dating disappointments, you're starting to think that nobody will be as good for you as your ex was.
- Even though you know he wasn't perfect, you really miss your ex and think he could have been The One. Maybe there's still hope.

- You've secretly started stalking him online, or driving by his house, or going to places (Starbucks, the bank, the grocery store) where you hope you'll run into him.

If the above behavior feels familiar, all signs point to the fact that you're still hung up on your ex. And you wonder why no one else has come along. There's no room for someone new in your life. Your first order of business is to knock your ex off the pedestal you've got him on. Start by once again getting realistic about who your ex really was, and why he wasn't—and still isn't—good for you. If needed, get out that pen and paper and make an honest to goodness *Reasons My Ex Sucks* list to reconnect to all the reasons he was wrong for you.

Once you do that, it'll be easy to see that putting him up on a pedestal is a huge mistake. (And worshiping him is only stalling your progress!) Right here and now, kick that pedestal over. Send your ex tumbling to the ground. And then imagine a black hole in the floor opening up and swallowing him. Once he's disappeared from view, make a pact with yourself to never again worship at the feet of a false idol. And the next time you meet a cutie, give him the benefit of the doubt. No, he's not your ex. Thank God!

The Great Wall of Whine-A

Okay, so you're definitely not pining for your ex or worshiping at his false idol feet. But before you throw yourself a fabulous *I'm so over my ex!* party, there are some other scenarios to consider. Yes, you're over him. But you may not be over the pain, hurt, and feelings of betrayal. In fact, you may be so *not* over it that you're convinced you'll never let anyone near your heart again. There's just one problem with this scenario.

On some level, you're letting your ex dictate your future. You may even think that by withholding your heart from every man you meet, you're somehow punishing your ex for his sins.

See, you're unconsciously saying, *You hurt me so much I'll never let anyone in again. That'll teach you!*

Now, if you're feeling a little defensive at the moment, there's good reason. You're most likely buying into this belief system that says by being so cynical, guarded, and/or emotionally unavailable, *you* win.

How's that working for you? Yes, you're keeping all those Mr. Nexts at bay. But you're not punishing your ex at all. In fact, he's probably already moved on and not paying any attention to you. (The truth hurts, doesn't it?)

from the *fearless female files* . . .

"I truly thought my ex was The One. But after seven months, and even though it is indescribably painful, I have finally turned the corner and given up on him. The problem is, I feel like I have also given up on love. I am able to channel my energy into work, but cannot seem to muster any hopefulness, enthusiasm, or belief that I will ever find anyone who I will love like I loved my ex. I'm an active, goal-oriented person who lives with gusto. But when it comes to love, I feel jaded, wounded, and cynical. I feel like something deep in my core has been lost forever."—amy

In trying to punish your ex, the only person who actually gets punished is you. By keeping your guard up, sealing your heart permanently shut, and shunning any potential suitors who happen to show up, you're blowing your chances at any form of happily ever after. What a shame!

Wouldn't it be better to forgive yourself for getting hurt? Wouldn't it be easier to let go of your need to punish your ex and instead step effortlessly into your blissful future?

The answer is yes. But until you're ready to ditch your drama, you're going to stay stuck, and only you can decide how long you want to be stuck for. A week? A month? A decade? The choice is yours. I suggest you get out your calendar, decide on an end date to your heart hostage situation, and get back to the business of your fabulous future.

Date-Ja-Vu

Here's another insidious way you may be still hung up on your ex and sabotaging your chances of meeting really great guys in the near future. Whenever you think about dating someone new and *really* getting to know them, the idea overwhelms you. If and when you find yourself on a second or third date with the same guy, you always find some random reason to get rid of him. Either he's too nice, too available, too into you—you name it. There's always a problem and a legitimate reason to jump to the dump.

Sound familiar, Dump-zilla?

Let me tell you what's really happening here. While you're allegedly making a valiant effort at the dating game, you're really just going through the motions. In all honesty, you don't want to get to know someone new. You have no desire to expend any energy or invest any time with all that getting-to-know-you verbal and emotional diarrhea. If—and only *if*—the universe would guarantee that you could have the exact same relationship you had with your ex with someone new and skip over the oh-so-important first few dates screening process, that would be perfect! Otherwise, you just don't have the time, energy, or interest, do you?

---

from the *fearless female files* . . .

"When I first started dating again, I was pretty terrible at it. I found any excuse not to see someone more than once or twice. Either his eyebrows were too bushy, or his car wasn't good enough, or he seemed too predictable. What was predictable was me. I ditched a lot of simply, truly nice guys because I was afraid of getting hurt again. Once I woke up to that painful truth, I had to get real. It was hard, but the best thing I ever did. Now I'm actually pretty good at dating. I even enjoy juggling several really great guys at the same time."—jeannie

---

If you're hoping to clone your last relationship with a brand new copycat relationship, I get it. I've been there. But guess what? Unlike Dolly the Sheep, your last relationship cannot be cloned. Nor should you want to clone it. If you put on your 20/20 hindsight glasses, you'll see that there were obvious problems and incompatibilities in your relationship. Like it or not, things didn't work out for many reasons. So why do you keep blowing off perfectly nice Mr. Nexts in favor of sitting at home and praying for a scientific miracle? Maybe you're not ready to get back out there. Maybe for the foreseeable future, you should take yourself off the market, focus on yourself and your own interests, and get more realistic about your last relationship. That way, when you're ready to start dating again, you'll be willing to invest the necessary time, energy, and enthusiasm to get the job done right. Oh, and to have a little fun along the way. As challenging as dating can sometimes seem, it's got to still feel fun for you to want to put yourself out there.

Martyr, Party of One

As you've been reading through this chapter, you may have felt a sense of relief knowing that you don't subscribe to any of the previous issues with your ex. In fact, you guys are still great friends. You managed to survive the breakup, help each other heal, and are now still actively involved in each other's lives. Impressive, to say the least!

So let me ask you something. Why haven't you moved on? Why aren't you dating someone new? Is it because you haven't met anyone amazing yet or because you're worried about how your ex would feel if you started dating again first?

Remember, brutal honesty.

If you find yourself thinking or saying, "Oh, I can't possibly go on a date yet. It's only been a few months!" watch out. By putting your ex's feelings before your own, you're setting yourself up for a serious setback once your ex starts dating. As magnanimous as you think you are, no one's that selfless. No one except a major martyr. And is that who you aspire to be? Someone who sacrifices her own success and happiness in hopes that her ex will miraculously meet someone amazing and move on first?

I don't think so!

Facebook Friends Weigh In

When I asked the question *Have you ever put off dating someone new in hopes that your ex would move on first?* on Facebook, here's what some of my fab friends said. . . .

"Yes, and then I figured out it was an excuse not to grow or be responsible for my own life. I didn't want to be the big martyr anymore—boring!"—JULIE

"Yes, but only because I wanted to get back with him and when he started dating someone else, that was more of a wakeup call that we were really over."—KATEE

"I put off dating someone new in the hopes my ex would drop the person they cheated on me with. Smart, huh? Looking back, it makes me sick when I think about all the time I wasted. At least I *finally* moved on."—DIANE

"In a word, no."—JOAN

When you review all of the possible ways you may be subconsciously holding on to your ex, what jumps out for you? How have you postponed your future by putting your ex on a pedestal, putting his needs first, or permanently constructing a wall around your heart? Regardless of how you've held on to your ex, and in the process put off meeting someone new, it's time to break free of this bogus behavior and embrace a new, healthier approach. One that celebrates the wise and wonderful woman you already are and continue to become. Whether you know it or not, it's time to get back out there. Even if you just dip a toe in the water and sign up for one online dating site this week, that's great progress! If you choose to be bold and dive in the deep end (online dating like a pro, attending singles events, and putting yourself in target-rich environments on a regular basis), even better! Or, if slowly but surely wading into the shallow end is more your style (e.g., going on one date this month), go for it. What's most important here is that you symbolically free yourself from any chains your past may still bond you to, and instead walk into the waiting arms of your perfect present and fabulous future.

1. Take a look at the scenarios illustrating how you may still be hung up on your ex. Allow yourself to get really honest and admit which scenario is holding you back.

2. Next, make a game plan for breaking free of those old chains and getting back out there. Will you start slow, signing up for online dating? Pick up the pace and put yourself in target-rich environments once a week? Or dive in and employ numerous dating tactics? Write down your game plan and be sure to include the dates by which you plan to implement each item. (This will keep you accountable.)

Share Your Results

Want to share your game plan with me? Join my Facebook fan page and let me know how you're breaking free from your old chains and getting back out there.

chapter 9

why you're really still single

Now, let's say you hired a therapist, matchmaker, or a relationship coach to help you overcome obstacles, let go of limiting blocks, and ultimately attract qualified candidates for the role of Mr. Next until you successfully call in Mr. Right. You'd invested time, money, and emotional energy into working with this person. What if they told you the exact same thing, that you're the real reason you're still single? What would you do? Initially, you may want to unload a piece of your not-so-diplomatic mind on them. But what would happen if, instead, you took their feedback as constructive, surrendered to the truth, looked them square in the eye, and asked, "What do I need to do to change the results I'm getting?"

Believe it or not, improving your chances of finding that dream relationship you want (or at least improving your dating results) is as simple as a   sking a better question. While it may be painful to face the truth—that you're contributing to your single status, as well as participating in all those unsatisfying relationships in your past—this is the next step in your romantic reinvention. By not coming from a place of ego, instead accepting that you may be the real reason you're still single, you change the course of your future. You may even cut down on wasted dating time with Mr. Wrong and ultimately snag yourself Mr. Right that much sooner, just for being open-minded about how you can change your relationship future.

Before we go any further, let's be clear about one thing. If you don't want a relationship, enjoy being single, and have no interest in finding, attracting, and enjoying your perfect partner, that's just fine. In fact, that's fabulous! Being clear about what you want is the first step in manifesting your ideal future. But if you're reading this book, I'm guessing that at some point in the future you'd like another relationship, hopefully a healthier and happier one. If so, my goal is to help you manifest your dreams.

Now, let's get back to business. Like it or not, on some level, you *are* participating in being single. Whether you enjoy being single or not, whether you want to meet the man of your dreams or not, whether you love your life or not, if you want a different result than what you're currently experiencing in *any* area of your savvy single life (and why else would you be reading this book?), you've got to ask a better question. You've got to let go of your ego (you may not even know she's rearing her fabulously ugly head), get really honest, and ask yourself and the world around you *What do I need to do differently?*

It's okay if you don't have any answers. That's what this book is for. In this chapter, you will learn four amazing secrets to transform your energy and outlook from *single and sorry* to *single and fabulous!* Even better, when you implement these secret strategies within your life, you'll dramatically increase your chances of meeting plenty of potential Mr. Nexts—everywhere and every day!

Secret #1: Expand Your Social Network

Conventional wisdom says that you are the sum of the five people you're closest to. These five people affect your level of happiness, success, abundance, and joy. Make a list of the five people you spend most of your free time with. Be sure to be completely honest with yourself.

Now, review your list. Who are your five people? Are they married or single? Male or female? Gay or straight? Happy or unhappy? How old are they? How do you typically spend time together? In one another's homes or out in the world around you?

Your answers may look something like this:

The five people I spend most of my free time with are:

1. My dog (While not technically a real person, your pet may in fact be one of your closest "friends." Be honest!).
2. My parents.
3. My married best friend and her family.
4. My gay best friend.
5. My coworkers (for the occasional after work cocktail).

Do you see how your single gal social life may unknowingly suffer? Sure, you have plans every weekend. But with whom? People who can celebrate your single status, help you meet men, and/or introduce you to new hot spots where available and interesting men are in abundance? Or people whose conversations center around colonoscopies, what happened this week on *Survivor,* and which cutie they hooked up with last weekend at the after hours club?

Review your list one more time. Can you see how your immediate social circle may be stifling your chances to meet

eligible men? Whether you spend every Saturday night with
your best girl friend and her family watching the latest arrivals
from Netflix, or only venture into social settings with your
fab gay friend, or spend every Sunday going to brunch with
the folks followed by napping with your cute pooch, take a
look at how little time you actually devote to putting yourself
out there and meeting eligible straight men. While it doesn't
need to be your full-time job, to get real (translation: *different*)
results you've to invest reasonable effort on a regular basis.
For example, dedicate at least three hours a week to breaking free from your current routine (AKA your dating desert,)
and put yourself out there. And by "out there," that means
you need to shower, pick a cute outfit, brush your hair, put on
some lip gloss, and leave your Bluetooth headset and/or iPod
at home. Get out into the world around you sans distraction.
Go to a bookstore on a Saturday afternoon and browse the
travel or technology section. Hang out at a coffee shop Sunday morning reading a book with a conversation-worthy title
(*Think and Grow Rich* is a good one!) and be on the lookout
for potential cuties. Or recruit your pooch to be your wing-
dog and head out for a day of hiking, hanging at the dog park,
or volunteering at a pet rescue organization, and so on. The
truth is, Mr. Right isn't going to magically show up on your
doorstep ready for a relationship with you. And if he did,
you'd swear he was a stalker, dial 9-1-1, and get a restraining
order. Right now, your mission is to step outside your comfort
zone, get out there, and work it—without your married best
friend and the baby stroller or your gay BFF who might look
like a boyfriend to the unsuspecting straight guy who thinks
you're cute and wishes you were available.

Now, I'm not asking you to give up the most important
people in your life. I'm just asking you to expand your social

circle enough so that they're not the *only* people you regularly socialize with.

Let me give you an example from my own life. Once upon a time I worked in Corporate America. It was a very family friendly environment and I was the token single girl. I absolutely loved my job and had the good fortune of working along side my two best girlfriends (both married with babies). I spent forty hours a week in an environment that celebrated family values. Not only that, but I also spent weekends with my girlfriends and their families. We went to dinner, went to the movies, had game nights, and so on. There was just one problem. I was perpetually single and absolutely flabbergasted about it.

Was I participating in being single? You bet! And it wasn't until I broadened my social circle, incorporating time in new environments with my single and fabulous gal pals that my social life shifted. I started Internet dating, went to networking events where I met and dated several really great guys, and learned to embrace life outside the married-with-children bubble I'd been living in as an imposter. Hallelujah!

As comfortable as you probably are in your current social life with your cozy friends, if you want to shift the level of success you're having when it comes to meeting and dating men, you've got to shift your social circle. Translation: You *must* meet and spend time with other single women. Not only that, but it's essential that you put yourself in target-rich environments on a regular basis. And when you see a cute guy? Instead of running the other way, meet his gaze, smile, and grant him permission to approach. Above all else, always leave your house looking super fresh and fab-u-lous!

Secret #2: Work It at Work!

Having been involved in my own workplace romance once upon a time, and having experienced the Big Breakup in the office, I don't advocate dating at work. What I *do* encourage is *working it* at work! Here's what I mean. If you work in an office building, there are probably people in your work environment who can help your dating efforts. For example, your fellow single male coworker who plays in an office basketball league (and knows tons of eligible single guys!), the fabulously single girl from marketing who always goes to the hottest singles spots (ask if you can tag along!), and/or the woman who's always organizing get-togethers outside of work. If she's super social, she most likely knows some single men!

Don't be afraid to enlist other people in your dating efforts. Start recruiting people you get along with to introduce you to great guys they may know as well as local singles hot spots you need to know about.

Of course, this *is* your work place. You don't want to be a walking personals ad. Practice subtlety and select your helpers wisely. If somebody is a huge office gossip, you most likely don't want to entrust them with fixing you up with their friends. Instead, choose your trusty assistants wisely, based on their ability to be discreet as well as their access to untapped groups of single men. Invite these helpers to lunch or grab a coffee and chat. Let them know you're single and looking. Ask them if they know any potential candidates they can introduce you to.

And not only should you start enlisting the help of your coworkers, but now's also the time to take off any self-imposed blinders and pay attention to potential dates outside your office but in your general vicinity. For example, the cutie you always bump into in the elevator in your building. Or the good-looking guy you always spot when ducking out for your latte fix. Or the sexy stranger who smiles at you whenever you're both picking up projects from the nearby copy center. Give yourself permission to make eye contact, smile, and flirt. Remember, you're single and ready to mingle! These are awesome opportunities to work it during your work day without dating *at* work. Woohoo!

Now, if you happen to be one of those lucky people who work from home, this may be a challenge for you. Without the aid of coworkers and an office environment, your chance to meet someone becomes more difficult.

I didn't say impossible. So before you mumble some excuse about how you'll be single and working from home in your pajamas forever, stop. Shower. Put on that sassy outfit in your closet just waiting to be worn, style your hair, apply a little makeup, and head out to a coffee shop at least once this week. Chances are, there's at least one or two work-related tasks you can do while sitting at a table sipping a cappuccino. And given the amount of people who work from home these days, a coffee shop can be quite the social scene for the savvy single!

Secret #3: Participate in Group Activities

Here's another great secret for expanding your social circle and opening yourself up to possibly meeting a new cutie or two. It's time to start participating in group activities. First, let's get specific about the kind of group activities I mean. Right now, your idea of group activities may be limited to your knitting circle (there's a reason they call these groups Stitch and Bitch), your group Weight Watchers meeting, or your yoga class. And while you enjoy those activities and should continue doing so, it's time to expand your horizons.

Open your mind and think about group activities that you might enjoy that would also include men. For example, if you've always wanted to learn how to sail, enroll in a sailing class at the local yacht club. Or if you love the outdoors, join your local Sierra Club and participate in organized activities like group hikes and camping trips. And if you're passionate about a particular cause that's near and dear to your heart, start volunteering. Again, let's target your results. Volunteering for a homeless women's shelter probably won't allow you to meet many (if any) single men. However, if that's the cause speaking to your heart, go for it. Try to pick a second cause where you might meet actual living, breathing men. Examples include an environmental group, a political action committee, and/or a Race for the Cure type organization benefiting an affliction that both men and women suffer from.

Caution: *Do not* join a cause or organization that goes against your beliefs just to meet a guy. The goal here is to choose a cause, event, or activity that's meaningful to you and also offers the potential to meet eligible men. That way, even if you don't meet Mr. Next, you're still doing something good for others and feeling good about yourself. Talk about a win-win!

Once you've found an organization or cause that's meaningful to you, the work begins. Your mission is to show up looking and feeling effortlessly fabulous and event-appropriate (i.e., a cocktail dress at a soup kitchen is so not the way to go). Channel your most confident self and introduce yourself to your fellow volunteers. Be open, friendly, and cooperative. And don't immediately make a beeline for the token cutie. Ultimately, the goal is to let your new acquaintances get to know you, like you, and eventually invest in your single gal efforts. You may not make a love connection instantly, but the people you meet may have single and interested friends, siblings, and coworkers. Remember, all you're doing right now is expanding your social circle, getting involved in your community, and recruiting your helpers wisely.

Secret #4: Get to Know Your Neighborhood

Take a step back from your living situation and assess your neighborhood. Do you live in a rural or urban area? Are the people in your neighborhood young, older, or mixed? When you walk around, are there other pedestrians? Is your neighborhood predominantly single, families, and/or both? Where you live can seriously affect your social life, both positively and negatively. I learned this firsthand.

While working in my family friendly office environment, I had the good fortune to buy my first home, a cute two-bedroom, two-bath condo a short commute from work. I fell in love with the condo because of its beautifully manicured grounds, the security of living in a gated community, the affordable price, and its close proximity to the office.

What I didn't factor in was the neighborhood. Shortly after moving in, I realized that I had relocated myself to suburbia. Everyone at the grocery store had a least one child in tow. All the restaurants nearby were family friendly. Even in my Pilates class the conversations centered around kids and Cub Scouts.

Once again, I was the odd girl out. Just like my job, my home life celebrated other people's life choices—marriage, babies, and minivans. There were no hot local singles' events, sexy pickup bars, or target-rich environments for me to explore.

Within a year, I rented out my condo, moved to my dream neighborhood—a very pedestrian friendly, singles-heavy, artsy bohemian environment—and within four months met my husband.

You may not need to move. Even if you do, you might not get the same results I did. But you owe it to yourself to take an honest assessment of your neighborhood. If you're the token single, you've got to make some changes. For example, identify neighboring singles-friendly communities that may help you meet like-minded (and available) men. Consider driving a few extra miles to go to a more singles-friendly grocery store, gas station, bank, or post office. Again, to get better results in your dating efforts, you've got to mix up your routine and regularly put yourself in single-and-ready-to-mingle environments.

In real estate, location is everything. The same is true in dating. Being geographically desirable can only boost your chances of snagging a great catch. Again, you don't have to move. You just need to incorporate some subtle, savvy single gal shifts into your life to make your dating life more geographically desirable.

1. Make a list of the five people you spend the most time with socially. Review the list. How are these people helping/hurting your ability to meet potential dates?

2. Starting today, make an action plan to expand your social circle, including more time with single female friends and/or more time in target-rich environments.

3. What organizations can you join that will help expand your social circle? Identify the events, activities, and groups you'll join, as well as a target date for joining them.

chapter 10

don't be that girl: dating personas that can sabotage your success

Now that you're really and truly over your ex and ready to get back out on the dating scene, it's time to break free of one last barrier. Starting today, you need to identify and release any negative, desperate, or otherwise unappealing personas that may show up with you on dates. Whether you know it or not, it's these personas that may be sabotaging your success. The following quiz will identify any dominant dysfunctional dating personas that show up on your dates, and offer insights into how you can release the drama and celebrate your inner queen.

Dating Persona Quiz

1.	When you meet a cute new guy, your first thought is:
	A. With the right haircut, wardrobe, and styling products, he could work.
	B. Are you kidding? *This* is all that's available?
	C. Great. A perfectly nice guy that I'll somehow screw it up with.
	D. He seems nervous. That's so cute! Let me put him at ease. . . .
	E. Nice car, good job, cute dimples. Hello, Prince Charming!

2.	When someone you're dating flakes, blows you off, or doesn't return your last call, you think:
	A. I can make him like me. Just watch. . . .
	B. Good riddance. That jerk wasn't good enough for me anyway. Did you see his shoes?
	C. I knew it. I'm such a mess that he couldn't handle me.
	D. He must have had a bad day. Why don't I just call and offer to make him dinner?
	E. He must not be The One. Oh well. . . .

3.	When the guy you've been seeing asks you to be exclusive, your initial reaction is:
	A. Excellent! We're right on schedule.
	B. Who does he think he is? I'm keeping my options open in case someone better comes along.
	C. Is he serious? Doesn't he know how unstable/insecure/screwed up I am?
	D. I'm going to be the best damned girlfriend *ever*!
	E. Woohoo! Happily ever after at last!

4.	When one of your girlfriends gets engaged, your response is:
	A. Better pick up the pace so we can be next!
	B. Sure, she's engaged. But look at the toad she's marrying!
	C. Great. Soon, everyone I know will be engaged and married. Except me.
	D. Maybe if I offer to buy the ring, he'll propose sooner. . . .
	E. She's so lucky! How'd she do it?

5.	Whenever anyone asks why you're still single, your response is:
	A. I've just been so busy with my career. Did I mention I got a promotion?
	B. There are no good men left. *Trust* me.
	C. My therapist thinks I have a fear of intimacy. She's probably right.
	D. I'm still getting over INSERT EX'S NAME. I mean, he's still sleeping on my couch so it's not like I can date anyone else.
	E. I have no idea. Why? Do you have someone you can set me up with?

Your Results
(And How They Affect Your Dating Life)

If you mostly answered A. . . .

You Are: The Shero

In the workplace, The Shero is an excellent planner, leader, and worker bee. She's highly detail-oriented, loves a challenge, and thrives in a fast-paced environment. However, when it comes to her personal life, these same traits may sabotage her chances at love.

If some or most of your quiz answers fit into the Shero category, don't despair. Many amazing women throughout history have been Sheroes: fabulously fierce females with highly expressed masculine energy. The goal isn't to destroy the Shero in you. It's to understand your inner Shero so that you can temper how she shows up in your love life.

Here's a little secret about men. They like to feel needed. They want to do things for you. Not because they have to, but because they actually want to! By being such a dominant force in a relationship (or even on a date), your inner Shero may intimidate even the strongest, most confident guy. If you're constantly taking charge, planning your dates down to the tiniest detail, insisting on going Dutch on every date, and in general making it loud and clear that you don't *need* a man, your date will get the picture. He'll most likely also take a hike, feeling emasculated, unnecessary, and unappreciated.

So what's a Shero to do? Lighten up. Understand that those amazing qualities that lend themselves to your professional success don't necessarily help you on a date. By learning to channel your softer side, letting your date take charge and shower you with attention, affection, and interest, and letting go of your need to loudly and proudly show the world how well you take care of yourself, you can rebalance your masculine and feminine energies and actually improve your dating results. You don't have to give up your day job, stop paying your bills the minute they arrive, or pretend you need rescuing. On the contrary. By being self-sufficient *and* appreciative of the little things a man can bring to your life, you embody your best self and attract the kind of man who will ultimately appreciate you.

If you mostly answered B. . . .

You Are: The Princess

Be honest. Are you used to getting your way all the time? Or worse, when you don't get your way, do you throw a silent or full-blown temper tantrum in hopes of swaying the results? While that may have been an acceptable response when you were two years old, it's very unattractive as an adult. And if you have a habit of resorting to such juvenile behavior, you may be a bit of a princess. Ironically, if you *are* a Princess, you may not see anything wrong with the label. However, it's time to wake up and smell the dating dysfunction.

Armed with a chip-resistant sense of entitlement, the Princess believes that the world revolves around her every want and need. (Again, a Princess personality may not see anything wrong with this.) But if some or most of your quiz answers fall under the Princess persona, here's how behaving badly affects your dating life: When the Princess persona is fully engaged, you scare off the good guys and instead attract men who gravitate toward drama, chaos, and, well, bitches. These guys tend to be doormats, which a Princess will happily walk all over until she gets bored. Then she'll ditch him like a bad habit in search of more exciting and dramatic dating prospects. During this phase, she'll fall for a suave bad boy (he may be a prince but he's definitely not a king!), drawn to his emotional unavailability. However, like a true Princess, she'll quickly get frustrated with his inability to cater to her every need. She'll then ditch the bad boy in search of another doormat, and so on.

The problem with this vicious cycle is that both sides of the spectrum are equally unfulfilling. Over time, the Princess will grow increasingly frustrated, convinced that no man will ever satisfy her. And she's right. That is, until she gets her entitlement complex in check, takes an honest assessment of her own bad behavior, and decides to make a change to a better choice. Armed with self-awareness and humility, the Princess can learn to attract a healthy and handsome guy who will treat her with respect and make an excellent partner. But first, she's got a lot of work to do. And it starts with letting go of her ridiculous demands, embracing the idea that a healthy and happy relationship is a two-way street, and that she has to check her diva ways at the door.

If you mostly answered C. . . .

You Are: The Bitter Babe

If the majority of your quiz answers fall under the Bitter Babe persona, the good news is you're not a lost cause. The not-so-good news is that you have some work to do before you'll really be ready to incorporate healthy dating habits and eventually find, attract, and keep Mr. Right. And since there's no time like the present, keep reading!

If your childhood was tumultuous, if your past dating life has been dramatic, and/or if you suffer from low self-esteem, it's all too easy to feel like a Bitter Babe. It's also incredibly tempting to believe that real and lasting love is only available to other people. While your fabulous friends seem to have no trouble meeting great guys who want to commit to them, you're convinced that the same opportunity will never come your way. Here's the problem with that belief system: It limits your level of success. It also sets you up to only attract a certain kind of guy, usually someone equally limited in thinking, emotionally stunted, and/or seriously dysfunctional. And while there are certain payoffs for this dead-end dating desert (you get to blame your parents for your lousy upbringing, prove to the world how screwed up you really are, and never take responsibility for your life in general, let alone your love life), it's so not the road to travel down.

Before you can attract a healthy and happy relationship into your life, you've got to let go of your identity as damaged goods. Regardless of how unhappy and/or unhealthy your childhood was, no matter how many times you've loved and lost, your future is not determined by your past but by your own belief system about what lies ahead for you. If you can imagine that your future holds beautiful, amazing, exceptional love, you can and will experience it. First, you've got to be willing to let go of what no longer works. Next, you've got to shift your belief system to see and embrace a new reality. Finally, you've got to take steps on a daily basis to manifest your new reality. Again, it is possible. Your job is to bring this new reality to life, step-by-step.

If you mostly answered D. . . .

You Are: The Caretaker

Are you a sucker for a slacker, aspiring artist, or other seemingly full of potential guy who just can't catch a break? If most of your answers fall into the caretaker category, then you most likely love nursing these broken-winged babes back to health. There's just one problem. Most of them never get healthy. So unless you enjoy the idea of taking care of your guy for the rest of your life, you need to change your behavior. Start by identifying exactly what it is that you get out of being a caretaker. What's in it for you?

Typically, caretakers crave the feeling of being wanted and needed. They like caring for their significant other because it makes them feel powerful and empowered. Truthfully, being a caretaker is a power trip. By having the upper hand over your hottie with a heart of gold, paying the bills, tending to his broken spirit, helping him through his emotional turmoil, you ensure his codependency and rest easy knowing he can never leave you.

But guess what? By committing to him, you abandon yourself. Forced to put his needs first forever, you slowly but surely begin losing pieces of the amazing woman you are at your core. You may not notice the loss at first because you're so busy being high on your power trip. But eventually, taking on a caretaker persona will exhaust you. It will rob you of your vitality. Over time, you'll start to feel resentful, maybe even bitter. And that just won't do. You deserve better than that. So why not quit while you're ahead? Before you become burdened with a lifelong lazy lad who sucks you mentally, emotionally, and spiritually dry, break free of your need to control and coddle. Learn to nurture and care for yourself. As you heal your inner power struggle (that's what it's really all about), you'll shift the kind of guy who shows up in your life, ultimately attracting a candidate who will love and support you as much as you love and support him.

If you mostly answered E. . . .

You Are: The Damsel in Distress

If the majority of your quiz responses fall into the Damsel in Distress persona, we've got some work to do before you can attract a realistic and healthy relationship. Quite the opposite of the Caretaker, the Damsel in Distress is the one in constant need of rescue. However, unlike the Bitter Babe persona, she doesn't necessarily feel bad about her mess. In fact, she thinks that it's perfectly okay to throw caution to the wind, live beyond her means, and avoid any sense of personal accountability because that's what a good providing husband will bring to the table. Unlike the Princess, she doesn't brazenly believe she's entitled to more than her fair share. She just can't be bothered to rescue herself. As a result, her finances are a mess and she hates everything from her job to her family. Yet, she does nothing to fix her situation, convinced that any day now, Prince Charming will show up and save the day. Again, it's not ego that drives her. It's just plain fact (as she sees it).

Sound familiar?

If you live your life like a Damsel in Distress, your attitude needs a major adjustment, or at least a reality check. Let's start by facing this harsh reality: If Prince Charming *did* show up on your doorstep, he'd take one look at the mess you've created and high tail it back into oblivion. No healthy, happy, actualized man wants anything to do with a woman who can't take care of herself. You don't have to be perfect, but you can't be a total mess.

So what's a Damsel in Distress to do?

First, take ownership of the mess you've created. Start by holding yourself accountable for the areas that most require your attention (e.g., delinquent debt, broken-down car, bad relationships with your parents). Next, work with the appropriate people to take the necessary steps to repair any neglectful damage. You don't have to have sparkling credit, a flashy car, or perfect parents to make a lasting love connection. But you do need to be as healthy as possible on your own fabulous two feet before thinking about inviting some guy into the picture. Plus, by taking personal responsibility for your life, repairing any major riffs or ruts, and rescuing yourself, you greatly increase your chances of wowing a really great guy, and eventually wooing Mr. Right. So go ahead, Damsel in Distress. Rescue yourself!

Don't Be This Girl Either: The Bitch

Before you discount the possibility that you may actually be one, the Bitch can fall into any of the previously mentioned personas. She's a dangerous character you'll want to avoid at all costs, as she leaves nothing but trouble in her wake. To see how the Bitch may be showing up for you, ask yourself the following questions:

1. Are you making any new guy you meet pay for the sins of the jerk who broke you heart?
2. Are you so critical of the men you date that there's no way they'll ever measure up to your impossible standards?
3. Do you believe that being difficult is just part of the test you put potential partners through to see if they can handle you?

4. Are you so afraid of getting hurt again that your best defense is an impenetrable emotional fortress?

5. Do you get off on making men work their asses off to please you, only to let them know in no uncertain terms that they've failed?

If you answered yes to any of the above questions, you most likely bring your inner Bitch with you on dates. The verdict? Time to give your inner girl behaving badly the boot!

Do you see how certain personas may be sabotaging your dating efforts? Whether your masculine energy is turned up too high (and making those men run for cover) or your desire to be rescued is repelling the good guys or you fall somewhere in between, it's time to release any unhealthy attachments to these precarious personas and instead become the most well-adjusted woman you can be. Remember, you don't have to be perfect to attract an amazing man, but you do need to heal any unhealthy emotional wounds, fix any blatantly irresponsible messes, and learn to let the great guys in your life audition for the part of leading man. When you do, you'll dramatically shift the romantic results you experience and ultimately enjoy dating so much more. Can I get a *woohoo!*?

1. When it comes to dating, which persona shows up most noticeably for you?

2. What do you need to do to let go of that persona and shift the results you're getting? Make a plan for change and implement it.

Got Questions?

Got questions about how to break free of the dating personas that sabotage your success? E-mail me at *ask@LisaSteadman .com*.

chapter 11

men behaving badly— guys you don't need to date

Now that you know the kind of women you shouldn't be in the dating trenches, it's time for your crash course in the boys to avoid. Whereas in the past, you may have wondered why your dating efforts were constantly thwarted by losers, players, and mama's boys, your dating present and future will be so much brighter because of the clarity you'll gain in this chapter. Once you can clearly identify the men who will only waste your time, stall your progress, and aren't worthy of inheriting the title of Mr. Next (let alone Mr. Right), you can quickly and easily steer clear of them and ultimately pave the way for a good guy to make his entrance.

Hurts So Good: Drama Kings to Dodge, Not Date

Whether you know it or not, you have a weakness for a certain kind of guy who's just not good for you. Don't worry. Until we wise up, every woman has at least one precarious predilection—the guys we fall for too fast, the ones who constantly disappoint us, and who are ultimately bad for our emotional well-being (even though they hurt so good). Let's take a look at the possible men you bend over backward for in hopes of breaking your bad habits once and for all.

The Addict

He may be really into you, but guess what? An addict will always love his addiction more. Your general fabulousness and love will never change that. So whether he's an alcoholic (they can have jobs, homes, and bank accounts and still be drunks), "just a pothead" (*I'll take rationalizations for 1000, Alex!*), or is addicted to prescription or street drugs, let's be clear. An addict is an addict. He will never choose you over his drug of choice. Nor will he ever change his ways simply because your love is strong. And even if you only suspect he has a problem, this little "problem" won't disappear on its own. Before you get in too deep emotionally, you need to face facts. It's not your job to fix or save an addict, no matter how cute, smart, or full of potential he may be. As romantic as it sounds, it's not sexy or realistic to pin your hopes on some guy who's already involved in a love affair with his substance of choice. By sticking around, you don't so much guarantee your happily ever after, as you do your happily never after. Get out while you can.

Famous Addicts

In the 1980s, we loved to save Corey Feldman and Corey Haim. In the 1990s, it was Robert Downey Jr. and Kurt Cobain. The 2000s brought problems for Colin Farrell, Nick Carter, and Mel Gibson. These guys are sexy, but definitely not worth your time and energy.

Bitter Boy

In the last chapter, I talked about the importance of healing old wounds so that you don't walk through life as a Bitter Babe. The same is true for Mr. Next. Whether you're a caretaker by nature or working to exorcise your own emotional demons, you don't have time to waste on a guy who holds on to his baggage like it's his life-support system. Repeat after me: Screwed up is so *not* sexy. To get better dating results, Mr. Next needs to be emotionally available, head and heart healthy, and traveling baggage light. That doesn't mean he has to have had a Beaver Cleaver childhood. It just means he's no longer overly burdened by the pain of his past. Whereas once upon a time, you might have felt the need to save a guy from himself, you now know how unsexy and unhealthy that dating reality really is. If and when a guy who believes he's permanently damaged presents himself to you on a date, take notice and steer clear.

Famous Bitter Boys

Andy Dick (also an addict), Dennis Rodman (another addict), and Shawn Stewart (Rod Stewart's reality show–hopping son—also struggling with addiction) are all notorious for their tendency to be (very) damaged goods.

The Player

The Player is the biggest and best-wrapped present under the tree on Christmas morning. It's bright, shiny, and eye-catching, but while you think it has your name on it, it's actually a gift for everyone. Or at least that's how the Player operates. He's smooth, sweet-talking, and has the uncanny ability to get women to go home with him. Once you're there? You're a lost cause. His bachelor pad is filled with toys, technology, and tools to woo and wow even the most practical woman. From his wall-to-wall flatscreen TV to the surround-sound speakers in every room to his impressive wine collection, the player is a master at playing. In fact, he's most likely a card-carrying member of the Peter Pan Club. And why should he grow up, settle down, and/or start a family? His lifestyle totally works for him. But will it work for you? Only temporarily.

Here's the tough love truth about the Player. He likes to have fun. He enjoys female companionship, but he never sticks with one companion for long. So while visiting his playground can be exhilarating and exciting, don't stick around, waiting for your monogrammed bathrobe. It's never going to happen. The Player will never wise up and change his ways for you. Instead, he'll just stop calling, texting, and pursuing you. He'll find a new bright and shiny object to play with. Ouch! While the Player can be a fun distraction, he shouldn't be a serious contender for the role of Mr. Next. In other words, next!

Famous Players

George Clooney is the ultimate player. Sure, we love to love him, but the trail of young beauties this leading man has ditched over the years is endless. In our fantasy, it'd be fun to be a contestant in George's Dating Game. In reality, the only parting gift is a broken heart. (And maybe he lets you keep the designer gowns from all those Hollywood parties.) Other famous players include John Mayer and Jamie Foxx. Cute, sexy, and fun, but commitment-shy, work-obsessed and emotionally unavailable, too.

The Slacker

On paper, The Slacker could never be a contender for Mr. Next, let alone Mr. Right. But then you meet him and he's charming, adorable, and full of potential. Suddenly, you find yourself making excuses for sticking around. *But he's so cute,* you start saying. Or, *He's got a great heart.* Or, *If he could just get his act together, he'd be a great catch!*

Stop right there.

While dating a slacker in college was cool, giving your heart to one now would be foolish. Back then, you weren't looking for a guy with long-term potential. Heck, you yourself probably only had a part-time job, slept till noon, and got to spend summers lounging poolside. A slacker made perfect sense in that scenario.

But now you're a grown-up. You have a job, responsibilities—an honest to goodness grown-up life. So before you travel too far down this dead-end road, ask yourself this: How much time are you willing to invest in a guy who has plenty of potential but no actual plans for follow through? It may sound harsh, but an even harsher reality would be falling for and committing to a guy who can't hold a job, who wants to move in immediately so he can save on rent, and who has no concept of saving for a rainy day, regardless of how much money he could potentially make some day as an artist, musician, or entrepreneur *if he could just catch a break.* Just as you can no longer afford to be the Damsel in Distress, you can't afford to waste time on the Dude in Distress. 'Nuff said.

Famous Slackers

Steve-O of *Jackass* and *Dancing with the Stars* fame is the classic slacker. Amusing? Yes. Fun to watch? Sure. But serious relationship material? Only if you don't easily tire of fart jokes and dutch ovens at bedtime.

The Sociopath

Here's the best way to spot a Sociopath on the dating scene: He comes on strong, charms the pants off you (sometimes literally!), tells you he's in love with you way too soon (even though it's nice to hear, it's not reality), and then once he's wormed his way into your heart, he destroys your life.

By definition, a Sociopath has no empathy or moral compass, which means that he cannot truly experience or give love. He can, however, appear charming, giving, loving, and generous, which makes him that much harder to spot. And while a Sociopath may woo you, wine you, dine you, and sixty-nine you, when his true colors emerge there is no denying how ugly and un-charming he really is. Whether he's telling you how to act, what to do, criticizing your actions, belittling your behavior, or lying, cheating, and stealing from you, one thing's certain. You want nothing to do with a Sociopath. If and when you sense a Sociopath is in your dating surroundings, run the other way—fast!

Famous Sociopaths

Ever hear of Ted Bundy? No, not Al Bundy, the lovable buffoon from *Married with Children*. Ted Bundy, the sociopathic serial killer. Obviously, not all Sociopaths are serial killers, but their destructive tendencies will slash away at your heart, confidence, and life as you once knew it.

The Workaholic

Just as you should get a certain level of satisfaction from your job, so should Mr. Next. But guess what? Any man who's married to his career most likely does not have the time or energy to make room for you. While it's great to date a guy who genuinely enjoys his job, it's more important to attract an individual who has a healthy work-life balance. That means he works hard forty to fifty hours a week, and also finds plenty of time to play, date, and relax.

So how do you tell the difference between a guy who's dedicated to his job and a guy who's married to the office? When you're on a date, does your guy:

1. Monopolize the conversation, talking about work?
2. Constantly check and respond to his BlackBerry?
3. Regularly take phone calls from the office?
4. Routinely cut your dates short so he can get back to his job?

If you answered yes to more than one of these scenarios, you're most likely dating a Workaholic. Before you commit to this career-obsessed cutie, you need to know all the facts. Regardless of what he tells you, his singularly focused ways won't change once he nabs that promotion or gets transferred to another division. And while the idea of settling down with someone who offers such financial security may be tempting, do you really want to spend birthdays, anniversaries, and weekends alone while your honey's off handling business? I don't think so.

Famous Workaholics

Justin Timberlake, Anderson Cooper, Anthony Bourdain, George Stephanopoulos, Ryan Seacrest . . . the list of famous workaholics goes on and on. When a man loves his job, it's a beautiful thing. But when he's married to his job? Run away—FAST!

The Emotionally Unavailable Man

Another guy you should avoid at all costs is the emotionally unavailable man. He can fit into any of the previously mentioned personas, so it may be hard to categorize him. On the surface, he can be fun-loving and fabulously good looking, but he's totally toxic to your emotional well-being! Here's how to spot an emotionally unavailable man on the dating scene:

1. He tells great jokes and loves to have fun, but doesn't reveal himself emotionally.
2. He doesn't ask a single getting-to-know-you type question—*ever*!
3. He gets a kick out of putting you down (even if it's done in a joking way).
4. He's the life of the party in his social circle but outside of it, he's most likely socially awkward.
5. Everything about his life shows you he's a chronic bachelor—he's perpetually single, has a lot of female friends, is always looking for a new and exciting experience, and never talks about long-term goals or plans (at least none that include a woman).

As you reviewed the men behaving badly, did you identify the ones you're most drawn to? Did you also see how being attracted to them may sabotage your success? Now's the time to break free of those bad boy habits and instead incorporate a healthier outlook on who Mr. Next can and should be, and who ultimately deserves the title of Mr. Right. When you're ready, move on to the next section and get a glimpse of a more promising dating future. . . .

Nice, Nice, Baby!

Now that you've stripped yourself of the need to save someone, suffer with, or struggle through another dead-end relationship with Mr. Wrong, it's time to embrace a healthier dating future. And the best man for the role of Mr. Next? Mr. Nice Guy. Now, before you scoff at the idea, and your inner critic tells you there are no amazing available men left, listen up. There are plenty of good guys out there. And now that you're free from those bad boy binoculars, you're going to be able to spot them in no time!

So where can you find these seemingly elusive good guys? Contrary to what you might think, they're not cowering in some mysterious cave on the island of Never Gonna Happen. But they're also not likely to walk right up to you, introduce themselves, and ask for your number. See, good guys can be shy. They can feel intimidated by all those players and slackers who for years have effortlessly swooped in and snagged the girls they were eyeing from across the room. While they *are* walking and breathing among us, they're subtler than their flashier counterparts you used to waste time with. In fact, if you're not paying attention, you can easily miss the good guys in your everyday life.

So what's a girl to do? Take off her blinders and take notice! The next time you're having drinks with your girlfriends, standing in the fifteen items or less line at the grocery store, or shopping for a USB drive at Best Buy, stop for a minute. Take a look around. Keep an eye out for the cutie in the corner who's shyly eyeing you. He most likely wants to meet you, but needs a little encouragement. Go ahead, make eye contact, offer a friendly smile, or if he's within earshot, simply say hello. By giving him a clear green light to approach, the good guy will most likely make his move. And when he does, give him plenty of encouragement in the form of continued eye contact, an enthusiastic head nod, and a little flirty laughter.

Remember, men—especially good guys who may not be brazen enough to regularly approach women they don't know—have a deep-seated fear of rejection. And if you shoot him down in his initial approach? He may not try again with someone else for months. So even if you realize he's not the guy for you, don't be cruel. Instead, let him down as easily as possible so that he can summon the strength to try again in the future.

Tips for Rejecting Good Guys

If and when you find yourself in the company of a good guy whose interest and affection you're just not digging, don't ditch him callously or become an abrasive bitch. Instead, let him down easily but firmly, taking a gentle *thanks but no thanks* approach such as:

- *I'm really flattered but just not looking to date right now. I'm sure you understand.*
- *You seem like a great guy, but I'm taking a break from the dating scene.*
- *Thank you so much for asking me out. I'm just not ready to get back out there yet.*

By being compassionate when turning someone down, you invite good dating karma to come your way in the future. By being a bitch? Look out! You never know when bad karma will strike back.

Top Ten Reasons to Give a Good Guy the Green Light

Not sure you're ready to hang up your bad boy habits? Take a look at the top ten reasons to change your ways and give good guys the green light.

1. Good guys call when they say they're going to (unlike those infuriatingly inconsistent bad boys).
2. Good guys are interested in you and your amazing life (and don't monopolize the conversation bragging about themselves).
3. Good guys like women and will treat you with respect.
4. Good guys can be great kissers.
5. Good guys save for a rainy day (making them great partners!).
6. Good guys like being in a monogamous, committed relationship.
7. Good guys make phenomenal fathers.
8. Good guys care about your feelings.

9. Good guys have passion (it just may be lurking below the surface).
10. Good guys let you finish first (*Hallelujah!*).

See how making the initial effort to call in these nice guys can reap major rewards down the road? And in case you need a little more convincing, here are some examples of fabulous and famous good guys. . . .

Seal: The guy writes and performs love songs for goodness sake. And have you ever seen Heidi Klum look happier?

Seal on the secret to marriage success: "What we do try and do is to keep everything fun, and I think in a funny way therein lies the key to romance, is the ability to always laugh and to find different ways of entertaining each other."

Danny Moder: Sure, Julia Roberts is famous for her smile, but since she met and married Mr. Moder, she's got the permagrin going on! And she's the first to credit her hubby with her happiness. Love that!

Julia on Danny: "I'm in the harbor of my life. Danny has really shined the light for me."

Hugh Jackman: He can sing, dance, act, *and* is a dedicated husband and father. Not to mention he's a super hottie. (Have you seen him without his shirt? The total good guy package — with pecs!)

Hugh on keeping his priorities straight: "If I didn't have [wife] Deb, I don't know if I'd have kept acting. With the risks, having someone's unconditional love means you can fall on your ass and be completely loved, even if the rest of the world chucks tomatoes at you. . . . And the same with kids. . . . If your career is more important than them, you're going to have hell. You see things get out of whack, out of balance, because they just mirror it back to you. To feel at the end of the day that you haven't done everything you could for your kids — none of it's worth it."

As you prepare to meet Mr. Next and eventually attract Mr. Right, it's important to assess who should and shouldn't be a contender for your time, energy, and emotions. If you have a track record of attracting men who can't meet your needs or consistently blow you off, it's time to break free of your predilection for these predators and instead remove your blinders so you can welcome the good guys in your environment. If they seem shy or uncertain, give them the green light so they can make their move. And remember, rejection is scary. If and when you decide a particular candidate isn't for you, gently throw him back in the water so another amazing woman can snag him when she's ready.

1. Review the list of Men Behaving Badly. Which ones are you most drawn to on the dating scene? How can you break free of the attraction to make way for better candidates?

2. In the past, have you dismissed good guys because they were too nice, available, attentive, and so on? If so, are you willing to once again give a good guy a try?

chapter 12

so you think you're relationship-ready . . .

Now that you've been schooled in why you're still single and what to do about it, how to avoid channeling your inner drama queen on dates, and the boys to avoid in your search for Mr. Right, it's time to regroup. To effortlessly attract Mr. Next, you need to next assess your overall relationship readiness. Whether your goal is to play the field, snag and bag a cutie, or settle down with your perfect partner and start a family, your success ultimately depends on how ready, willing, and able you are to dump any lingering unhealthy habits and channel your most authentic and amazing self. What follows are ten important measures of relationship readiness. By becoming a master in all areas, you'll be ten steps closer to dating nirvana and well on your way to calling in Mr. Right.

Factor #1: You Know What You Want

The very first step in understanding if you're heart healthy and ready for real results is to ask yourself just how clear your vision of the future is.

Now would be a good time to check in with yourself and ask these important questions:

- What is it that I want in life and love?
- Can I clearly envision myself experiencing this kind of life and love?
- Do I believe I deserve to have a beautiful life and be in blissful love? If not, what am I willing to do to change how I feel about my self worth and my ability to manifest real love into my life?

Attracting the right potential partners and eventually the real love deal begins with a simple step—understanding exactly what you want to call in. Once you're clear about your vision of your ideal dating goals and/or relationship results—how love feels, what healthy and happy relationships look like, who you are in a fun and fabulous relationship—it will be so much easier to invite it into your life. So starting today, honor your healed heart by asking yourself what your new and improved version of happily ever after looks like. You can best capture your new vision by doing the following:

1. Write it down. Consistently revisit what you want and refine your picture by writing about it in a journal.
2. Create a vision board. Collect images, words, phrases, and photographs of your ideal relationship future. Assemble them on a poster board and place your vision board in a high-traffic area of your home so you regularly see it, experience it, and have a reminder of what you're looking to manifest.
3. Meditate on it. Spend time sitting in silence and visiting your romantic future. By not only seeing what you desire,

but connecting to it regularly, you effortlessly call it in to reality.

Factor #2: You've Identified and Refined Your Requirements

Whether it's written down or not, you most likely have a long, detailed list in your head about who this Mr. Right is. You want a guy that's handsome, tall, has wavy hair, doesn't have too much body hair, likes sushi, isn't a mama's boy, rides a motorcycle, and is Jewish. While those superficial desires and wishful laundry lists are fun to make, they're not actually going to help you get clear about who could be right for you. Do you know what's *genuinely* important in attracting your perfect partner? It's time to get specific about the traits and qualities that *will* be right for you in your perfect partner. And that's where this next factor comes in. You need to define your relationship requirements. Unlike those fun but sometimes frivolous wants and needs I mentioned earlier, your requirements are non-negotiable. Translation: Your potential partner *must* possess these qualities before you'll even consider dating him.

By writing down your relationship requirements (which you'll be doing at the end of this chapter), you gain clarity about the kind of person you're looking to attract who will not only be a great catch, but could also possibly be perfect for you. Then, when you're in the dating trenches and Mr. Next reveals himself as not being in alignment with those requirements, it's easy for you to walk away and never look back because you know that without those requirements, a relationship wouldn't work anyway. Talk about cutting down on wasted time!

To help illustrate the difference between relationship wants and requirements, here are some examples:

LIST OF POSSIBLE WANTS

- Six feet tall (at least).
- Blue eyes.
- Makes $100,000+/year.
- Loves to ski.
- Speaks French fluently.

While the attributes on this list are exciting and specific, they don't in any way give you the measure of the man who possesses them. Read on to see how this next list of potential requirements shifts the identity of Mr. Right into crystal clarity.

LIST OF POTENTIAL REQUIREMENTS

- Lives well within his means.
- Doesn't smoke.
- Wants children.
- Is in good health.
- Loves to travel.

Do you see the difference? While you may find yourself most attracted to tall men with blue eyes, unless you absolutely refuse to date someone who doesn't match these qualities (and how limiting is that?), they are more of a want or desire than a requirement. On the other hand, if finding a partner whose financial fitness (regardless of annual income) is important to you, then living well within his means *is* a non-negotiable requirement on your list. And when you meet a tall guy who's up to his baby blues in debt? You won't date him because his financial fitness doesn't match your relationship requirements (regardless of how super cute he is!). It's not a tough call to make. It's the only call you *can* make.

So go ahead and make a list of at least ten of your relationship requirements. You can even start by making a larger list of all the wants, needs, and desires you hope to find in a mate. When you're done, divide them into three categories:

1. Relationship requirements (those must-have deal breakers).
2. Wants (nice to have but not absolutely necessary).
3. Needs (Traits that rock your world but that you're willing to compromise on for the right guy. You may not know these are negotiable until you meet a great guy without them.)

By separating your list of traits, qualities, and desires into these three categories, you open your eyes to what's absolutely essential for you to find in your perfect partner, as well as what may have once seemed important but is now more superficial or unnecessary. And once you're clear about what you absolutely *must* have from Mr. Next, it will be that much easier to manifest him into your reality. Love that!

Factor #3: You're Happy and Successful Being Single

When it comes to being single, are you in the Woohoo! camp or the Boohoo! camp? Here's how to tell the difference. You're in the Woohoo! camp if you make the most of your savvy single life, know how to have fun on your own terms, and enjoy the freedom being single affords you. On the flip side, if you feel lonely, miserable, and desperate to put your single days behind you, you're more likely in the Boohoo! camp.

Savvy singles in the Woohoo! camp tend to have a healthy outlook about being single, as well as an optimistic view of the future. Singles in the Boohoo! camp are also known to hate their job, resent their friends' happiness, have dysfunctional relationships with family members, and walk around with a bad attitude about their life in general. If you find yourself in the Boohoo! camp, it's no surprise you're still single. Like it or not, the key to attracting a healthy and happy man is to become healthy and happy on your own first. Then and only then are you truly relationship-ready.

If you find yourself struggling to feel satisfied with your life right now, it's okay. You're not the first fab female to feel frustrated by lackluster dating results, suffer from an overwhelming desire to be married and have children by now, and experience discomfort watching all your friends marry and settle down while you can't even snag a second date. Here's the deal: By wearing that frustration on your sleeve, you repel any potential cuties from coming your way. Plus, you give off the impression that you're desperate for love, which is so not sexy and repels Mr. Next!

Earning your Boohoo! camp badge isn't worthy of your time or energy. If at all possible, take steps to turn the volume down on your frustration and do your best to live and love your life, starting today. Here are some tips to help shift your feelings about being single and earn yourself a rightful place in the Woohoo! camp:

- Make fun and fabulous plans for your upcoming weekend. Be sure to include well-deserved pampering (a spa appointment), time with your fellow single girlfriends in places chock full of dating prospects (bars, clubs, and parties rather than stitch and bitch gatherings), and a leisure activity your ex would have hated that you absolutely love.

- Splurge on a symbol of your single status that can be a reminder to love your life as it is right now (weekly fresh flowers to brighten your home, a silky robe you wear around the house to feel fab, or those diamond stud earrings you've been coveting).

- If your social life revolves around friends who are married with children, expand it to include some healthy and happy single gal pals who love their lives, too. If all your friends are happily hooked up, you may need to make some new friends (more on this later).

- Shake up your routine at least three times during the week by putting yourself in new environments (stop for an after work cocktail with coworkers at the upscale bar near your office, attend an interesting lecture, art exhibit, or book signing on a Thursday night looking your super sassiest, or join a co-ed softball league that plays every Saturday, for example).

- Get out of your comfort zone and say hello to at least one cute stranger every day (the cutie looking at wine at Trader Joes, the mystery man smiling at you across the bookstore, the potential Mr. Next you bump into while in line for popcorn at the movies).

You'll be surprised at how making these subtle shifts in your emotional energy and weekly routine will change how you feel about being single. Additionally, you'll shift the kind of guys who are attracted to you, and soon enough, you'll have plenty of Mr. Nexts to choose from!

Factor #4: You're Ready and Available for Commitment

While you may *think* you're ready to find, attract, and experience dating and relationship bliss, you may unconsciously be carrying around truckloads of emotional baggage from previous relationships. The downside? You sabotage your dating efforts. To once and for all become baggage light, start by assessing what baggage you may still be holding on to. Are you:

- Still blaming and shaming yourself for past relationship mistakes?
- Still hung up on a past relationship, unable or unwilling to let anyone new into your heart?
- Punishing every guy you meet for your ex's sins and in general sabotaging your chances of finding love?

Take an honest inventory of your emotional baggage. Is there excess weight holding you back? And if so, are you willing to do something about it?

Once you've assessed your emotional baggage, it's time to dump it. Here's how.

- Forgive yourself for whatever mistakes you feel you made in the past. Whether you stayed too long in the wrong relationship, sacrificed too much of yourself to Mr. Wrong, or feel like you were totally betrayed by love, now's the time to forgive yourself.
- Understand that you cannot change what's already happened. All you can do is move forward fearlessly. So right here and now, let yourself off the hook for any past relationship regrets.

If self-forgiveness isn't the issue, you may have some bitter baggage to dump. This can be trickier because you may also be in denial about it.

Here's how to tell if you're lugging around too much bitter baggage:

- You were so hurt by a past relationship that you've made it your life's mission to share your story of betrayal, disappointment, and drama with everyone you meet, including the new men in your life (ever notice how fast they run away when you do?).
- You're so convinced that love is a big, fat, untrustworthy lie that you've constructed an electric fence around your heart and no one gets in—or out—alive.
- When one of your friends, family members, or coworkers gets engaged, married, or has a baby, you secretly (and cynically) wait for it to blow up in her pretty little face. If it does, you smirk and feel justified in your cynicism and bitterness.

Sound familiar? While bitterness and cynicism may have been great company during your post-breakup cocoon, they're not the kind of BFFs you want hanging around for the rest of your life. Do yourself a favor and dump those bad habits ASAP. Here's how:

- Give yourself permission to trust again.
- Let go of your need to be bitter and jaded and, instead, practice healthy (and daily) doses of optimism and possibility.
- Accept that you may have made poor choices in past relationships and in honor of your healed heart, pledge to do

better in the future when it comes to attracting suitable Mr. Nexts.

- Make a pact with your healed heart to become a red flag specialist. As soon as Mr. Next's behavior triggers your internal alarm system, act accordingly and walk away.
- Understand that dating disappointment is part of the game. Learn to differentiate between disappointment and actual heartbreak. For example, if and when some guy you just started dating stands you up, doesn't return your last call, or decides to go back to his ex, there will of course be feelings of disappointment. However, you weren't emotionally invested enough for actual heartbreak to occur. In fact, your heart shouldn't get hurt until you actually exchange *I love yous* with someone really special who could be Mr. Right. If and when the guy you're in a committed and loving relationship with stands you up, doesn't return your last call, or decides to go back to his ex, that's when actual heartbreak may occur. By understanding the difference between disappointment and heartbreak, you'll be better able to navigate the tricky dating terrain.

By dumping any leftover emotional baggage, you will undoubtedly feel lighter, freer, and more open to the possibility that love can and will find you again. Additionally, you'll most likely discover that your schedule opens up and that shaking up your routine on a regular basis can be fun and oh-so-fabulous. Don't stress if the process takes time. Contrary to popular belief, miracles *don't* happen overnight. They take time, effort, and energy. (And besides, what else did you have planned for the rest of your life?)

Readiness Factor #5: You Have a Healthy Attitude about Your Work

While it may not seem like a direct link to your love life, how you feel about your job and/or career path can have an impact on your relationship readiness. See, if you love what you do, find personal satisfaction in doing your job well, and don't allow your job to interfere with your schedule or ability to meet and date men, you're more likely to achieve relationship success.

If, on the other hand, you regularly put in overtime, work odd hours, feel miserable about your job prospects, and/or find your job incredibly stressful, you most likely don't have a lot of time, energy, or desire to go out and meet potential dates, attract healthy and happy men, and ultimately call in a satisfying relationship.

If you're currently unsatisfied with your work life, you may need to make a change before you can invite love into your life. Here are some possible solutions:

- Actively seek out a new job in the same field, request a schedule change, or launch a whole new career.
- Ask yourself what it is you don't like about your job and see if you can adjust your attitude so you feel better about going to work.
- Talk to your boss or take other steps to alleviate work-related stress.
- Commit to fitting one new social activity into your during-the-week routine.

By feeling better about your work and its environment and creating a lifestyle outside of the office that you genuinely enjoy, you make yourself more available for dating and relationship success. Plus, you become a whole lot more fun to be around, making you even more irresistible to men! By consistently committing to this important step, you ensure relationship readiness.

Factor #6: You Are Healthy in Mind, Body, and Spirit

So many women worry about needing to lose weight before they can meet Mr. Next. But they focus much less on their overall health, wellness, and well-being. Being healthy in mind, body, and spirit is what really makes you relationship-ready. If you suffer from chronic pain, mental illness, and/or some other debilitating health challenge, maintaining a lasting and loving relationship may be a struggle. That doesn't mean if you *do* have some kind of chronic condition, you don't deserve to find love. But on the journey toward happily ever after, it's important to assess your physical, mental, and emotional health. If something feels askew, honor yourself by working toward a healthy solution. As needed, start eating more nutritious foods. Exercise more frequently. Seek professional help for any physical or mental unease. Practice self-nurturing behavior. By feeling consistently healthy and happy, you give yourself the green light to meet Mr. Next and eventually attract Mr. Right.

Factor #7: Your Finances Are in Order

This can be a particularly touchy subject for some women, so pay attention if the subject would normally have you running for the hills (or at least retreating under the covers). If you've been waiting for a man to fix your financial or legal woes, now's the time for a reality check.

By perpetually putting yourself in a financial bind (e.g., you're overwhelmed with debt or ignoring/avoiding a legal matter), you live in denial. And that just won't do! Not only is it *not* your future partner's job to fix your legal or financial worries, but the sooner you clean up any unfinished messes, the sooner he can actually arrive. Starting today, take steps to consolidate those credit cards, face your financial and/or legal woes, and create a path toward resolution (even if the process scares you to death). It's the only way for you to step into your future and invite Mr. Next along for the ride. If you need help, consult a financial advisor and/or a legal expert, and together, take steps toward a more secure future.

Factor #8: Your Family Relationships Are Healthy

Before you can become 100 percent relationship-ready, you need to make sure your existing relationships are as healthy and happy as possible. Start by taking a personal inventory of your close relationships. Are they functional, emotionally healthy, and mature? Or are they combative, dysfunctional, and dramatic?

Whether you know it or not, having unhealthy and unhappy relationships with your friends, family members, and/or extended family can and will eventually interfere with your romantic life, and even sabotage a real relationship. That's why it's essential to your blissful future to repair any damaged relationships you have or at least do your best to heal old wounds. You may not be able to resolve everything (especially with unwilling, unhealthy, or unavailable individuals), but by taking steps and doing your part, you show the universe that you're willing to try. Not only that, but you also step up and choose to no longer be a victim of your past. The Mr. Nexts who show up as a result of your commitment to healthy and happy relationships will be equally healthy and happy on their own. Woohoo!

Factor #9: You Have Healthy Dating Skills

This next relationship readiness skill may require some practice on your part. And that's absolutely fabulous (and oh so fun)! To ensure future dating and relationship success, it's essential that you study, embody, and master the habits of effective and savvy singles.

Here are just some of the new skills you'll want to acquire.

You're Comfortable Initiating Contact with Cuties

In the past, you may have gotten tongue tied or even run the other way when you met a potential cutie. As a healthy and happy single, now's the time to become a seasoned pro at working it! That means whenever you find yourself in the presence of a potential Mr. Next (whether at a bar, a networking event, or even walking down the street), you feel secure enough in your own skin to make eye contact, smile, and say hello. This simple gesture will let him know you're interested, available, and confident. If he makes the next move, great! If he hangs back and you're feeling especially bold, strike up a conversation. He'll take the hint. The rest is up to him. And if he doesn't jump at your bait, no worries. You're self-aware enough to realize that it's his loss and you easily move on to the next potential cutie. No wasted time for you!

You're Comfortable with No Meaning No

If and when you find yourself on a date or in the presence of a potential date and it's clear that Mr. Next isn't a suitable suitor, you easily and effortlessly walk away, no hard feelings. This is especially important when your date exhibits unhealthy, dysfunctional, or bizarre behavior (e.g., hostility toward his ex, extreme jealousy or rage, and/or any other display of emotional instability). Rather than hop on his emotional roller coaster and ride until you're dizzy, you're able to recognize the warning signs, politely but firmly extricate yourself from his environment, and walk away with your head held high, knowing you're far too fabulous to get involved with someone who could be hazardous to your heart.

You Effortlessly Handle Rejection

If rejection is part of the dating game (and it is), then you can't let yourself get bogged down every time a date doesn't result in a love connection. Instead, your job is to handle any dating disappointment you experience with style, class, and ease. Not only are you adept at celebrating your successes, but you're also the queen of letting go of any dating drama, disasters, or disappointments. Plus, you've mastered your own flirting and dating style, become a successful attraction magnet, and are always on the lookout for Mr. Next. Talk about a winning strategy!

You Keep Your Physical and Emotional Boundaries Intact

In the past, you may have jumped into a physical relationship too fast because of the chemistry between you and Mr. Wrong. Or maybe you revealed too much too soon emotionally on a date and things quickly fizzled. As a healthy dater, you now have boundaries in place so that physical intimacy never progresses too quickly, and an emotional connection is built over time rather than too quickly with someone you barely know. By establishing, communicating, and maintaining your boundaries on the dating scene, you teach all those Mr. Nexts what's appropriate and how you'd like to be treated. If and when he disrespects those boundaries, you comfortably (and without drama) call him on it and decide if he deserves another chance or if it's time to move on.

Factor #10: You Have Healthy Relationship Skills

After mastering the skills of being a savvy single, your next order of business in becoming relationship-ready is to study and master long-term relationship skills. Here are just some of the relationship skills you will want to become adept at.

You Effortlessly Maintain Intimacy with Your Partner

Establishing healthy intimacy between two people requires that both individuals are self-aware and comfortable expressing themselves and their needs with their partner. Once intimacy has been established, maintaining it becomes the next challenge. To effortlessly maintain intimacy, both participants must be consistently ready, willing, and able to reveal their most authentic selves, be vulnerable when necessary, and stay emotionally connected with their partner even in times of stress or crisis. If and when a problem arises, both partners must come together to reestablish intimacy. While it may sound daunting, it can also be the most worthwhile connection you ever make with someone.

You're Comfortable Communicating Your Needs

Healthy, long-term relationships are built on a strong foundation of open communication. That means to successfully attract and keep Mr. Right, you must master the art of communicating your needs in healthy and appropriate ways.

Start by getting clear about what your needs are. Communicate these needs to your partner in healthy, appropriate ways. Honor your partner by listening to his needs in return. Effective communication includes being up front about how you feel, and listening and sharing in a reciprocal manner. Don't expect your partner to be able to read your mind. And whenever possible, avoid using emotional blackmail, issuing ultimatums, or engaging in unnecessary arguments just to get your needs met. When you master this skill set, you will have mastered the art of healthy relating. Mr. Right will thank you!

You Allow Yourself to Trust and Be Vulnerable

One of the most fulfilling rewards of being in a healthy partnership is the ability to completely reveal yourself to your loved one. This requires a level of trust and vulnerability that can only be earned over time. Once you've achieved it, it's up to you to maintain this level of trust and vulnerability. How? By staying open, honest, and communicative. By consistently being aware of your thoughts, feelings, and energy, and by being willing to share that with your partner and receive his energy in return. By respecting your partner and his choices, as well as trusting that he has your best interests at heart and will never take advantage of your emotional vulnerability. By giving and receiving love without barriers or blocks, you open yourself up to a richer relationship than you may have ever experienced before. It may feel unsteady, uncertain, and scary at first, but it's so worth your time and effort.

So there you have it. Ten relationship readiness factors that contribute to your success on the dating (and mating) scene. By mastering these ten areas of your life, you embody your best self and guarantee a successful relationship future. Keep in mind that these skills may take time and practice. If there are specific areas you feel challenged by, don't expect over-night success. Instead, keep at it, practice patience, and work toward experiencing exceptional and consistent results.

1. Review the ten factors of relationship readiness. Which areas do you feel confident in? Which areas need the most work?

2. Create an action plan for improving your weak points and celebrating your strengths.

3. Regularly review your relationship readiness until you are satisfied with your skills and abilities.

the new rules of dating

Now that you're ready to brave the dating trenches, are you wondering if your social skills are up to date or *so five years ago*? Regardless of how long it's been since you were last single, it's time to enroll in a crash course in the new rules of dating. Before you skip over this chapter, thinking you already know everything you need to, think again. With all of the technology available to us and 24/7 access to instant gratification via Facebook and Twitter, the multitude of online dating sites, and the growing popularity of sexting (sending racy pics to the opposite sex via cell phone), dating can sometimes feel frustrating, confusing, and baffling. And with good reason.

Unlike the days when the rules were clearly and easily defined (a guy asked you out, you got to know one another, you decided to go steady, settle down, and eventually got married), you may not fully understand how dating has changed in the new millennium, let alone how you can play to win. What follows are the brand-spanking-new rules of dating. When you learn to embrace them, your results will dramatically shift from so-so to sensational. Soon enough, your winning strategy will win over plenty of potential Mr. Nexts, and in time, maybe even score you Mr. Right. Class is now in session!

Rule #1: Multi-Dating Is Easy, Affordable, and Essential

In the not-so-distant past, online dating made it easier to have a date on Saturday night. If you were lucky, you met someone great, and possibly fell in love. Today, the savviest singles know that dating is a numbers game. Instead of putting all your emotional eggs in one basket, multi-dating is the way to go. When you consistently multi-date, you free yourself from the pressure of making any one date with any one guy perfect. As a result, your expectations are more realistic because you know that if one cutie gets away, another will take his place. How fabulous is that?!

Plus, by multi-dating you get to put your flirting, dating, and mating skills to the test on a consistent basis with a variety of interesting, educated, and available men. By analyzing the results (i.e., your date's reaction), you can tweak your behavior, minimize what doesn't work (being too talkative, texting him too much between dates, and so on), and amplify what does (keeping his interest by being moderately mysterious, not sleeping with him too soon, and so on). Plus, by becoming a seasoned multi-dater, you get to sample the buffet of available men, decide what qualities and traits best fit your wants and needs, and eventually attract the most perfect catch for you.

Struggling to find one date let alone multiple dates? To get started, you've got to take off those self-imposed blinders and step outside your comfort zone. Before you freeze up with intimidation, you're not stepping into these new murky waters alone. What follows are five foolproof strategies for navigating the unexplored territory of multi-dating.

1. Sign up for multiple online dating sites and devote at least one hour a week to each site (updating your headline, profile, perusing the possibilities, and sending flirts or winks).
2. Find out about singles events in your area like speed dating, lock and key, and other mingle-friendly mixers, and regularly attend looking your flirty best (Do yourself a favor and learn how to work a room!).
3. Tell your friends that you're ready to get back into the dating trenches and ask if they know anyone they could introduce you to (if they say yes, hold them accountable for the introduction).
4. Enlist the help of a matchmaker who has access to an entire database of available, interested, and exciting prospects.
5. Put yourself in target-rich environments on a regular basis (be sure you look cute and make eye contact with any potential sweeties you see!).

And don't stop after posting your profile, attending your first singles event, or finding new singles hot spots you enjoy. Your new part-time job is to regularly put all of the previously mentioned methods into practice. When you do, you'll likely attract a handful of eligible candidates. Then it's up to you to multi-date with confidence. Again, the goal here isn't to commit to the first prospect you come in contact with. It's to get comfortable seeing and dating a variety of men so that you can make better choices about who you may eventually settle down with. In the meantime, relax, have fun, and enjoy!

Dating on a budget? You don't have to break the bank to be a successful multi-dater. And yes, that means men aren't expected to pick up the dating tab anymore. If they offer, graciously accept but don't expect it. You have a job, too! And to keep multi-dating within your means, mix up how you meet men, what you do on dates, and focus on shorter, more activity-oriented dates, including . . .

The Coffee Date: A first date really doesn't need to be any longer than an hour. Arrange to meet for coffee at a laid back, non-noisy coffee house. Arrive a few minutes early, order your latte or iced tea, and park yourself at the perfect table, preferably in a tucked away corner so the two of you can get to know one another without feeling like you're on display.

The Sports Date: If you and your date initially bond over sports (in your profile, over e-mail, via text, on the phone), make your first date a sporting event. Go to a baseball, hockey, or football game where you can continue bonding over bad calls, stolen bases, and frustrating fumbles (as well as exciting scores and winning the game), all without the pressure of those initial interrogation-style getting to know you questions.

The Active Date: A great way to get to know someone new is to strap on the roller blades, chalk up your pool cue, or slip into those rented bowling shoes. Whether it's your first time, or you're a seasoned pro, this can be a comfort zone–pushing experience that opens you up, lets your hair down, and ultimately makes you and your date more likely to reveal your true selves to one another. Just do   sore loser or an in-your-face winner. *So* not attractive!

The Group Date: Not ready for a one-on-one encounter? Invite the new guy to participate in a group activity like game night or softball. By being surrounded by people you know and care about, you're all the more likely to reveal your best self, while letting the guy get a glimpse into your world. Chances are good that if he can hang with your friends, he's probably a good prospect for a second date!

As you can see, gone are the days of dinner and a movie on the first date. In today's thoroughly modern world, first dates should be short, activity driven, budget-friendly, and ultimately allow you to get to know one another in a pressure-light environment.

Rule #2: People Have Shorter Attention Spans (In Other Words, Learn to *Work It!*)

Remember when conventional wisdom blamed MTV for creating the short attention spans of teens and tweens in the 1990s? Today, MTV seems like dial up compared to all the other high-speed outlets vying for our attention at any given time. From video games to 24/7 e-mail delivered directly to your iPhone or BlackBerry, to keeping up on your friends' lives moment by moment via Facebook and Twitter, it's growing more and more challenging to not only *get* someone's attention, but to *keep* it. So how does that apply to your dating efforts?

In all brutal honesty, it's not enough anymore to be a cute catch who's available. You've got to be a cute, clever, cutting-edge catch who knows where her target market is and how to reach them. That means you've got to get in the social media game, create eye-catching online dating profile headlines that you routinely update, and market your savvy single assets like a seasoned pro. Sound impossible? It's not. It just takes a little extra time, energy, and dedication. If you're committed to getting real results, you'll make the effort. You'll also reap the rewards—plenty of online and offline interest that translates into spark-inducing dates and, eventually, a relationship with Mr. Right. The following are tried and true strategies to make a splash in today's techno-savvy dating world.

Strategy #1: Social Network Like a Pro

The best way to capture attention in the social networking arena is to make consistent and compelling updates to what you're doing on your profile pages. Instead of simply typing "ate yummy pasta for dinner" or "went out for drinks with the girls," make your life more juicy with updates like "Made angel hair pasta tonight with freshly grated mozzarella, opened a bottle of Pinot Grigio, and am polishing off a piece of chocolate mousse cake. Dessert, anyone?" or "Sipping champagne with my Girls @ The Standard while checking out the cuties. Where do you go to make new friends?"

Do you see the difference in how and what you're communicating? By getting specific, you paint a vivid picture of your amazing life. That makes it so much easier for the Mr. Nexts of the world to take a peek and decide if they'd like to become a part of it. Then it's up to him (and him, and him) to approach, and for you to decide if he's worthy of crashing the party, AKA your life.

Strategy #2: Change Your Routine

Once upon a time, waiting for Prince Charming to show up on your doorstep seemed like a good idea. In the new millennium, who's got time to sit around and wait? To maximize your relationship results in today's fast-paced environment, you've got to learn how to work your single-and-ready-to-mingle status into your daily routine. Instead of just going to and from work every day, change your routine frequently (forget weekly, think daily!). That means whenever you leave your house you should look your flirty best, dressed in something cute and eye-catching. It also means you should mix up your daily routine, breezing into Starbucks to get your morning latte rather than relying on the drive thru even though it's quicker, going to the dog park looking super sassy (heels and your little black dress won't do, but how 'bout stylish sneeks, an eye-catching tee, and bootylicious jeans?), and instead of eating your lunch at your desk like you've been doing for months, get outside for some fresh air in a park while enjoying your chicken tarragon sandwich, or grab a fellow single coworker and hang out at a local lunch hot spot?

While you're in these new environments, keep your eyes peeled for potential cuties. Make eye contact, smile, and if possible, find a casual way to connect. Need examples? At a dog par, mention you're thinking about getting a bulldog and ask if he knows of any good bulldog rescue organizations. At the café, scope out the possibilities, choose a target, and approach with casual confidence, asking what time it is, if you can borrow the pepper, and/or what he's eating that looks and smells so delicious. Remember, getting a guy's attention isn't rocket science. It's a numbers game, and you've got to be in it to win it. Plus, most single guys are *dying* for an invitation to meet a cute girl. If you give them an opening, they'll take it (if they're smart).

Rule #3: Technology Has Changed the Game (*Embrace* That!)

Gone are the days of creating a clever online dating profile, uploading your fave photo, and sitting back, relaxing while the winks, flirts, and interest poured in. Today, the Internet dating pool is large and multifaceted. You now have to work a little harder to get real results. Invest in your success by embracing the multiple platforms now available to the average dater. From dating on multiple sites with specific target markets to adding video of yourself to your profile to giving online video speed dating a try, now's the time to explore your options, test the results, and see what happens.

To maximize your online dating results, review the following guidelines.

Join a Variety of Online Dating Sites for Maximum Results

Cover the spectrum of niche markets including one marriage-minded site if that's your goal (eHarmony.com and PerfectMatch.com are the most popular), one casual dating site (think Match.com, Chemistry.com, and so on), and one special interest site. Examples of special interest sites include

JDate.com (for Jewish daters), DateMyPet.com (for passionate pet owners), GreenFriends.com (catering to vegetarian and animal rights–oriented singles), BikerKiss.com (for motorcycle enthusiasts), and LargeAndLovely.com (for plus-sized daters) to name a few. By expanding your online dating search beyond just one site, and targeting specific areas of interest, you'll improve your search results and become a seasoned multi-dater in no time.

Create Specific and Compelling Online Dating Screen Names

Just like those intriguing updates you post on Facebook and Twitter, you need to create vivid, eye-popping, and captivating online dating screen names to enjoy better results. Remember, there are millions of daters out there vying for attention. To get your fair share of the action, make sure your screen name sparkles and shines! And be specific depending on the site. For example, on DateMyPet.com, instead of a generic screen name like "Jessie123" choose a more captivating screen name like "PugLover4U" or "BeagleBaby." On a casual dating site like Match.com or Chemistry.com, choose a screen name like "Flirty&Fab," "FunLovingLaura," or "PrincessLeia LookAlike." For obvious reasons, avoid negative monikers like "ManEater," "HardToGet," or "LoveEmNLeaveEm."

Make Sure Your Headline Reflects Your Intentions

Moving on to your online dating profile headline, they, too, will differ depending on the dating site you're on. However, each one should be eye-catching *and* reflective of your dating intentions. Instead of simply stating "Looking for love," or "Seeking my soul mate," make your headline sizzle with specifics.

Examples of effective headlines include:

- Flirty, fun-loving brunette seeks great guy who loves to laugh
- Attractive adventure junkie looking for bungee-jumping gentleman
- World music lover on the lookout for Groove Armada guy
- Francophile interested in meeting fellow wine, travel, and language enthusiast
- (Young) Katherine Hepburn lookalike seeking Bogart babe

Are you getting the picture?

Post a Variety of Flattering Photos

And speaking of pictures, make sure you post a variety of recent flattering and flirty photos on each of your online dating profiles. Like it or not, men are visual creatures and it's up to you to showcase your fab self in the best possible light. Here are some tips to help you choose just the right photos for your online dating endeavors.

Do: Post relevant pics on relevant sites (no shots of you being a bridesmaid on Chemistry.com, no Mardis Gras party pics on PerfectMatch.com, and be sure to capture you in your niche activity of choice on those specific sites—show your full curvy body shot on LargeAndLovely.com, your pooch *and* you on DateMyPet.com, or your fave photo of you straddling your hog on BikerKiss.com). Trust me on this one. Your results will quadruple (at least!) when you provide a variety of photos featuring you living and loving your life.

Don't: Post outdated photos where you felt more attractive or thinner, or include cropped pics where your ex's arm is the only thing left of his former self. No one wants to feel disposable and/or replaced. And when you leave an ex's appendage in the pic? Your potential date gets a visual of what may lay in store for him. (Just don't do it!)

Hate every single photo you've *ever* taken? You're not the only one. But here's the tough love truth about online dating. More is more. And rather than post just one super cute shot of you looking your absolute best, embrace the wonderfully imperfect creature that you are and flaunt your fab self with multiple pics in multiple settings—for example, posed, candid, indoor, outdoor, activity-driven, and glamorous. Just as with your screen name and headlines, the more specific you get, the better results you'll experience.

You may even want to invest in having professional headshots taken. Do whatever it takes to paint the ideal picture of who you really are.

On a budget? You can get quality headshots taken for under $300. Ask friends for references or look online. Think of the minor expense as an investment in your happily-ever-after future. In those terms, it's a small price to pay to attract Mr. Next.

Regularly Update Your Headline, Photos, and Videos

To get the best online dating results, you'll want to routinely post new photos, videos, and updates to your profile. This will move your profile to the top in online dating search results and help you attract the interest of the newest daters on each site. Plus, it shows that you're currently active on the site, which alerts those hot candidates known as Mr. Next that they should reach out and say hello while you're still on the market. Going, going, gone!

Rule #4: Dating Is an Industry

Since you were last on the dating scene, the dating industry has evolved into a sophisticated social science. There are hundreds of books dedicated to the art of online dating, how to snag and bag a good guy, and what rules to follow to ensure the man of your dreams proposes within the first year of dating. There are also coaches and experts dedicated to your success. As a savvy single, your job is to employ as many of the methods and professionals as you find useful, master the new principles, and date accordingly. Think of your dating life as a fun and fabulous part-time job. You need to implement the right tools, strategies, and support staff to make your job easier and more fun, and produce the results you want.

Before you scoff at the idea of paying someone to help you become a more effective dater, let me ask you this. Have you ever solicited the services of a hair stylist, manicurist, tailor, dentist, nutritionist, personal trainer, and/or financial planner? If so, you probably sought these people out to help you manage a task you *could have* done on your own but felt more comfortable enlisting the assistance of a trained professional. Thanks to their help, the results you achieved were most likely far superior to what you would have experienced by yourself. The same is true in the dating world. If you were happy with the results you were already getting, you wouldn't be reading this book, right? The following are some potential members you may want to add to your success team.

A Dating Coach

For the sake of full disclosure, I should state for the record that I'm a dating coach. But I don't recommend a dating coach simply because that's what I do for a living. I encourage you to consider hiring a dating coach because, like the personal trainer who helps you tone and tighten your body, the right dating coach will help you refine and strengthen your dating skills, producing remarkable results. A dating coach can work with you to:

1. Identify your relationship requirements (non-negotiables) as well as wants and needs so you're clear about the kind of guys you want to attract.
2. Get clear about your limiting beliefs and how to release them.
3. Understand potential dating traps and how to avoid them.
4. Analyze your dating and mating behavior and offer suggestions on how to improve your results.
5. Refine your dating skills to become a truly successful multi-dater.

An Online Dating Profile Expert

Believe it or not, there are people in cyberspace whose job it is to help you maximize your online dating results. When you enlist their help, they finesse your online dating screen name, headline, profile body copy, photos, and search results. They also coach you on how to make the most of online dating in general. Talk about a valuable service! If this interests you, do a Google search for online dating help or see if any of the dating sites you're on recommend a profile expert for added support.

A Matchmaker

When it comes down to it, do you worry that your lack of satisfying dating results stems from your lack of trust in yourself and your choices? If so, stop worrying. You can actually hire help to ensure you make more educated decisions in the dating game. An effective matchmaker not only possesses a database of eligible candidates, but she helps screen them based on your requirements, wants, needs, and desires. A worthy team player indeed!

If you feel overwhelmed with choices right now, stop. Take a deep breath. Rest easy knowing that at this very moment, you don't have to assemble an entire dating staff or meet Mr. Right by next week. All you need to do is open your mind to the possibilities and when you're ready, start implementing the strategies presented in this chapter. Even if you take it one step at a time, you'll make progress and achieve better dating results.

1. Review the new rules of dating. Which one can you implement this week? Create an action plan for doing so.

2. Invite your Woohoo Crew over for a brainstorming session. Help each other create cute, catchy, compelling screen names and headlines for each of the online dating sites you've joined.

3. Make a list of the members on your dream dating success team. Look into hiring at least one new team member in the next month.

Additional Support

Want more information on how you can work with me? Go to IfHesNotTheOneWhoIs.com/coach for details.

the secrets of scoring (dates!)

Now that you're relationship-ready, and have been schooled in the new rules of dating in today's techno-savvy world, it's time to unlock some oh-so-important success secrets. See, while online dating, singles events, and technology may have made it easier to meet potential Mr. Nexts, these dating advances haven't necessarily made it easier to connect and/or leave a lasting impression. (Some savvy singles would say they've made it even harder!) If establishing and maintaining a connection with Mr. Next isn't as easy as it used to be, how do you rock your first impression on those first few dates? Read on to unlock the secrets that'll have you effortlessly snagging and bagging multiple dates with multiple cuties in no time.

Secret #1: Be Yourself

When you meet someone new, especially someone super cute that you could be really into, follow this very simple rule: Be yourself. What, you were hoping to unlock the secret to eternal beauty, youth, and man-magnetism? Sorry to burst your bubble. It really is as simple as that. To ensure you make that memorable first impression and leave him wanting another date, here are some guidelines for mastering the art of being Y-O-U:

1. When you leave your house in the morning, always wear something that makes you feel comfortable and cute. That way, if and when you find yourself face to face with a hottie, you'll feel confident enough to smile, say hello, and wait to see if a connection is born.

2. When it comes to those first few dates with Mr. Next, plan fab and fun activities leading up to the date so that you're not spending hours and hours stressing or obsessing about every little detail. For example, have brunch and a mani-pedi gabfest with the girls prior to meeting Mr. Next for drinks that night. Or, enjoy a spa day with your gal pals, getting a relaxing massage and/or facial before showering, slipping into a super cute ensemble, and grabbing a cup of coffee with the cutie you met in line at Starbucks.

3. On the first date, show up a few minutes early. Scan the location, pick a cozy and comfortable spot, and double check that there's no lipstick on your teeth before striking a cute and casual pose. (If you can't be early, at least be on time. Nothing guarantees a bad first impression quite like showing up late, breathless and stressed.)

4. During the initial encounter, always be prepared with a few topics of conversation or ice breakers. Yes, Mr. Next should know how to carry on a conversation. But when in doubt, you can put him at ease, make him laugh, and/or turn an awkward silence into witty banter. (He'll most likely thank you later—and be all the more likely to ask for a second date!)

Secret #2: Have Fun

While meeting someone new and going out on those first few dates can be nerve-racking, it should also be fun. You heard me—fun! So instead of worrying about *where this might be going*, sit back, relax, and give yourself permission to be your most fabulous self. That involves maintaining eye contact, smiling when appropriate, and engaging your date in casual conversation (not grilling him about his job security, relationship history, and credit report). There will be plenty of time to assess long-term compatibility if and when you decide to continue seeing one another. But on those first few dates? Flirt a little and just have fun!

Need help figuring out how to infuse those getting-to-know-you dates with fun? Here are some guidelines.

1. Don't try too hard. Just as you can probably tell when a guy is trying too hard on a date, guys can also pick up on any negative vibes you're putting off. From desperation to anxiety to bitterness to still harboring feelings for your ex, you may be unknowingly sharing more than you think. And nothing's a bigger turn off to a guy than a fumbling, bumbling date who's trying way too hard to impress him. Just don't do it!

2. Have a sense of humor (and be willing to laugh at yourself). Let's be clear. Dating isn't always funny. But by maintaining your sense of humor while in the dating trenches, you'll score big time points with Mr. Next. When asked about past dating blunders, instead of rattling off a list of the losers, jerks, and exes who did you wrong, simply smile, laugh, and share a lighthearted story or two. Your date will appreciate your honesty and perspective. Plus, he'll most

likely share a funny story or two of his own. Together, you can laugh about the perils and perks of being savvy singles while also breaking the ice and genuinely getting to know one another.

3. Pick appropriate dating activities. Whether you're ready to get married and settle down or are content to perpetually play the field, be sure your first few dates with any guy are short, casual, and very public. For example, coffee shops, wine bars, and low-key cafes are great locations to meet and get to know one another. On the flip side, first and second date no-nos to avoid include meeting for a candlelit dinner at a fancy restaurant (way too serious and expensive!), spending the date at your home or his (never invite someone into your home or agree to meet at someone else's home until you've established a comfort level and trust), letting your date pick you up at your place and drive you to your date (no escape route in case he's a jerk), and/or an overnight trip away (there will be plenty of time for that later). Again, the first few dates with anyone are for slowly but surely getting to know them. Then, if you mutually decide you want to continue seeing each other, you can revisit the idea of a romantic dinner, spending time in each other's homes, and eventually going away together.

4. *Relax!* If you suffer from first- and second-date jitters, this guideline is especially important. Dating should be fun and fabulous, not stressful and stroke-inducing. The best way to represent yourself on a date is by being relaxed, comfortable, and easygoing. If and when anxiety rears its ugly head? First, ask yourself if there's a reason for the anxiety. Does your date make you feel ill at ease? Is his behavior rude, offensive, or demeaning to you or to the people around you (waiters, the valet, bartenders)? If so, you may need to

excuse yourself and get the heck out of there. You should always trust your instincts. However, if you're anxious by nature, it's important to find ways to calm down so that you can actually enjoy dating instead of fearing it. Nobody wants to date a tightly wound stress case. So practice deep breathing and just relax. If you suspect you have serious issues with anxiety, seek professional help.

Secret #3: Turn Down Your Inner Critic

The purpose of going on those first few dates with Mr. Next is not to decide if you want to marry the person seated across from you at the bar, coffee house, or restaurant. It's to discern whether they're worthy of another date. So do yourself a favor and instead of obsessing about what went wrong on your last date or worrying about whether or not this particular cutie may be The One, turn down your inner critic and just enjoy getting to know Mr. Next. Here's how:

Ask questions, and actually *listen* to his responses. Share things about yourself that are genuine in hopes of helping Mr. Next decide if he would like a second date with you as well. Withhold any judgment while on the date. This is *your* opportunity to absorb not only what your date says, but also how he says it, as well as how he listens to and responds to you. If you spend the entire date in your own head with your inner critic, analyzing, judging, and criticizing ("His haircut is *terrible!*" "Did you see the car he drove up in? Crap mobile!" "What kind of man doesn't pull out a woman's chair when they sit at a table? He's history!" "Look how nervous he seems. What a loser!"), you'll miss out on the chance to actually get to know this less-than-perfect person who could be perfect for you.

If your inner critic is loud, obnoxious, and the alpha female in your brain, the notion of turning down her volume may seem practically impossible. But it's not. See, it's not about pretending your inner critic doesn't exist. It's about acknowledging that she's a part of you, and making peace with her. Then when you're on a date and she rears her ugly bratty head, you simply sit back, smile, and tell her to shut up. The two of you can powwow about the date later. But while on the date, *you're* the one in charge. And you're going to practice a kinder, gentler approach to getting to know Mr. Next in hopes of better determining if he could one day be Mr. Right.

Let me give you an example from my own life. Once upon a time, my inner critic ruled my dating life. I picked apart perfectly nice guys on a regular basis. Here are just some of the reasons my inner critic vetoed some really great candidates:

He's nice, sweet, and emotionally available? What's wrong with him?

Flowers on a first date? He's trying way too hard!

He wants to split the check? Next!

God, he's calling way too much. Doesn't he have a life?

That shirt looks ridiculous on him. What was he thinking?

Now, you may agree or disagree with any of the above dating criticisms. And what feels right for you on the dating scene will be different than what's right for someone else. The reason I give these examples is that in hindsight, I realized that I cast aside some truly terrific men because of my own inner critic and insecurities. I also give these examples because along the way, something in me shifted. My inner critic and I called a truce. We agreed to sometimes disagree.

Then something amazing happened.

I started having fun on dates. I allowed myself the opportunity to meet, date, and enjoy getting to know a variety of interesting men. Sometimes we only had one date. Sometimes we dated for a couple months. But by turning down the volume on my inner critic and withholding judgment until there were clear signs of incompatibility, I was better able to get to know the men I dated. They were able to get to know me better, too. In the process, we allowed one another to make the most educated choices about whether or not we wanted to continue seeing each other.

Guess what else happened? When a sweet, smart, super cute Mr. Next captured my attention one summer night at my favorite local music lounge, I paid attention. And even though my inner critic was there, pointing out how young he looked, when he asked for my number at the end of the night I gave it to him. And when he called the very next day, I turned down the voice that snapped *He's waaay too eager!*, and instead accepted his invitation to dinner. When Mr. Next showed up for our first date with flowers and dressed in slacks, a sweater, and shiny shoes, my inner critic bristled. She snarled, *He's trying too hard!* and *He looks too straight-laced for us!* Instead of agreeing with her, I gently told her to shut up.

On our first date, this sweet man who was five years my junior (*Didn't we swear off younger men?* my inner critic wailed.) told me about how he'd gone to Paris the year before, even though he'd lost his job six months before the trip (*Not very practical!* she cattily pointed out.). He explained that even while on unemployment, he'd been able to save $200 a month for six months, and with the free miles he had earned while traveling for work at that job he'd lost, he was able to get a free round trip ticket AND a free week at a plush hotel in Paris. (My inner critic promptly shut up.)

Somewhere between Mr. Next's passionate account of Paris, his refreshing candor about how he worried about his little sister who was half his age and struggling in school, and turning to me at the hip music club we found ourselves at after dinner and telling me how much he liked my nose (*My nose? No one has ever liked my nose before!*), I realized something. Mr. Next was pretty fantastic. And if I didn't allow myself to get to know him better, it would be my loss.

Mr. Next eventually became Mr. Right, and is now my husband. To this day, my inner critic and I agree on only one thing—it's a good thing she shut up on those early dates and let me get to know him.

from the *fearless female files* . . .

"My ex was a real charmer. Charismatic, fun, the life of the party. But in private, he was moody, drank too much, and was never there for me when I needed him. After we broke up and I started dating other people, I realized that I was drawn to a certain type of guy. The Larger Than Life guy. I didn't feel good about myself around these guys. I felt ugly, unworthy, and needy, and they played into that because it worked for them. Then I met this new guy. Smart, laid back, sweet. He liked me, pursued me, and made time for me. And while he wasn't as outgoing as other guys I had dated, he had so many other fantastic qualities that I decided to give him a chance. Now, we're in a relationship and it's amazing! Thank God I broke that bad boy habit and wised up."—andrea

Secret #4: Leave Your Date Wanting More

The best way to snag a second, third, and fourth date? Leave Mr. Next wanting more! Regardless of how much fun you're having and how attracted you feel toward your date, keep in mind that men love the thrill of the chase. And if you give up all the goods right away or reveal too much too soon, he'll quickly lose interest and move on to someone else. Here's how to leave Mr. Next wanting more.

Keep those first few dates short and fun. Even if you really want to, resist the temptation to extend a date beyond the original plans. By having an exit strategy while things are still stimulating, you peak your date's interest and guarantee he'll ask you out again. For example, when he asks if you'd like to go for dinner after your coffee date, simply smile, say thanks, and offer up, "Some other time." Then walk away from the date knowing that he'll most likely be arranging that "some other time" soon (if he didn't already)! Next time, if he once again tries to extend the date, accept his invitation but only by an hour or two. As your dates continue, give him more access to you and your time as you feel comfortable. He'll enjoy the rewards and you'll continue feeling like the object of desire.

Just as you want to leave Mr. Next wanting more of your time on those first few dates, leave him wanting more physically, too. While you may feel hot and bothered for him, bottle up that passion for now. There will be plenty of time down the road to get your groove on. In the initial getting-to-know-you stages, a few passionate kisses should be all that you exchange. As frustrating as this dating rule may feel, it's essential to your overall success. The truth is, if you let a physical relationship progress too quickly, you ruin the chances of ever letting emotional intimacy develop. You also cloud your judgment and run the risk of falling into the sex trap, a tricky predicament that fools you into thinking that your sexual compatibility makes you a perfect match in all areas.

——— *Dating Danger:* ———
Avoid Emotional Sluttiness

Another secret when it comes to leaving Mr. Next wanting more? Avoid being emotionally slutty. Here is an example of appropriate versus inappropriate first date topics:

Appropriate: Where you grew up, what you do for a living, your hobbies, and what you're passionate about.

Inappropriate: How many sexual partners you've had, the many ways your ex was a jerk, how your parents really screwed you up, how much you hate being single and just want to get married.

Remember, the purpose of the first few dates is not to tell your entire life story. Rather, it's to provide a brief and honest glimpse of the incredible person you are and the amazing life you have so that Mr. Next can decide if he wants to know more (and vice versa!). By providing a sneak peek into your world, and keeping a tight lid on the rest of your fabulousness, you capture his interest and ensure that Mr. Next will be dialing your digits and asking you out again. Score!

Secret #5: Don't Play Games

Like it or not, dating is a game. Once you're schooled in the rules and guidelines, you can pick and choose what works for you and become a master. Having said that, this next tip may feel counterintuitive. While dating is a game, you shouldn't play games with the men you date.

How do you differentiate between playing the dating game and playing with your dates?

Dating itself is a game and there are guidelines to follow that will ensure greater success while in the dating trenches (this book is filled with them). Playing games with the men you date is mean-spirited and will only invite bad karma to visit you.

The best way to avoid playing games while dating is to be absolutely genuine with your intentions and actions. If you're interested in seeing Mr. Next again, say so. But if you're not, don't string him along with the promise of a call that you'll never actually make. And if Mr. Next calls or e-mails you, practice common courtesy and respond promptly, regardless of whether or not you'd like to see him again. Be direct and honest while also being kind. After all, you never know when you'll be on the receiving end of a similar call. And if you both agree to another date? Success! If not, pick yourself up, dust yourself off, and get back in the game. You don't have the luxury of time to get sidelined by each and every dating drama, disaster, or disappointment that comes your way.

If and when someone plays you? Don't use it as ammunition to take it out on the next person you date. That's a total waste of your time and energy, not to mention Mr. Next's emotions.

1. Review the five secrets of securing future dates. Which one will you incorporate on your next date?

2. Which secret do you find the most challenging? Chances are, it's the one that you need to unlock and practice the most. Challenge yourself to put it into practice on your next date.

3. How has your inner critic possibly sabotaged past dates? Make a list of criticisms she's made that haven't helped your efforts. Have a conversation with her and gently tell her to shut up.

Let's Connect

Share your progress with me! Join my Facebook fan page to let me know how you're enjoying the book.

chapter 15

the laws
of attraction

When it comes to meeting Mr. Next, getting to know each other, and trying to decide whether to dump him or jump him, attraction plays a major role. And while attraction is an important ingredient in the recipe for healthy relationships, it should never be the key ingredient. In fact, attraction can often lead you astray, convincing you that the chemical reaction you have to Mr. Next means that he's Mr. Right when, in reality, there's so much more to it. What follows are four important laws of attraction. By understanding and following these laws, you'll be better able to masterfully attract Mr. Next, steering clear of any Mr. Wrongs who would do nothing more than cause an unwanted chemical reaction along the way, and ultimately call in Mr. Right.

Law of Attraction #1: Understand the "It" Factor

One of my clients, Andrea, asked me the following question:

"This guy that I've been on a few dates is truly a good person, has great follow-through, and is really doing all the right actions. My question is with regards to physical attraction. It isn't that I'm not attracted to him, but I don't have the initial 'umph' that I had with my ex. I don't want it to be shallow or seem like I'm not looking for the 'real' attributes in a guy but I would hate to sacrifice the butterfly feeling. Do you often find women for whom the physical attraction developed later and if so do you have any thoughts?"

One of the most common questions I'm asked as a relationship coach is about the initial chemistry between two people. Specifically, my clients want to know if that initial spark of chemistry isn't there, is something wrong? And, more importantly, if it's not there in an instant, can the spark grow over time?

My answer is always the same. No. Yes. And then again, maybe.

Think back to the times when you've had the strongest chemical attraction to a guy. If you've had it, you *know* it. Whether you were in a committed relationship with him, just hooking up, just dating, or just friends, you remember the feelings. The sensations went something like this: instant, electric, unexplainable, butterfly-inducing, and crazy-making.

You heard me—crazy-making. See, when you feel something that strongly for someone, logic, reason, and rationale go out the window. In its place, you find yourself strapped in tightly on a hormonal and emotional rollercoaster that hurtles you up, down, inside out, upside down, and backward.

Exciting? Yes. Tumultuous? For sure. And guess what else? Nauseating.

And let's be honest. A relationship that makes you nauseous won't work for very long.

So let me ask you. When you look back at past rollercoaster romances, how long did the intensity last? If it was platonic/unrequited, it may have lasted quite a while. After all, there's something so intoxicating about unrequited lust. However, it's a dangerous addiction you'll want to break before you can actually attract a real relationship. (For details on how to kick unrequited love to the curb, keep reading.)

If it was romantic, how long did you stay on the rollercoaster ride? A month? Six months? A year? Probably depends on your tolerance for drama and trauma (not to mention head rushes).

The intoxicating thing about having an immediate and intense chemical connection with someone new is that it makes you feel sexy, alive, desired, and inspired. The excruciating truth reveals itself over time as you wake up to the reality that the initial spark you thought was enough to keep the relationship alive actually blinded you from a laundry list of incompatibilities. And when the relationship fizzled? It left hot, painful, smoldering ashes in its wake. Ouch!

Here's the real deal when it comes to attraction. Immediate and intense physical chemistry is *not* the foundation for a healthy and lasting relationship. If and when you feel something that strongly with someone you just met, you may want to consider running for the hills. Wait. Scratch the *may*. You *need* to run as fast as you can away from Mr. Wrong. That is, unless you enjoy cleaning up nuclear waste, which is what will eventually implode in your heart and spill over into every area of your life with the wrong guy. What a mess!

Okay, you're thinking. *If instant and electric connection isn't the stuff of lasting relationships, what is?*

Emotional intimacy. Shared values. Mutual respect. And a desire to share more than just a romp between the sheets with someone. A genuine need to spend your time, energy, and emotion on someone. These are qualities that develop over time. And when they do, they lead to physical intimacy, a passionate connection, and a healthy dose of hormones.

To the untrained eye/novice dater, this kind of getting to know you intimacy may not be as exciting or intoxicating as those rollercoaster butterflies, but if your version of happily ever after includes a lasting, loving relationship, it's an emotional and intellectual shift you need to make. Right now.

Remember this. An instant spark leads to uncontrollable flames, which lead to an emotional inferno that all too quickly burns to the ground. But a slow spark built over time has a foundation. It leads to a sturdy and steady flame of attraction that has the potential to burn brightly for years to come. And that can be oh-so-hot.

Law of Attraction #2: Identify *How Soon Is Too Soon?*

One of my clients, Jane, asked me the following question:

"One of my biggest fears about dating again is figuring out the whole intimacy thing. I mean, how soon is too soon? And how will I know? Help!"

Another common question I get from my clients, especially the ones who are back on the dating scene after *years* in the wrong relationship, is about sex. Specifically, when to have it with someone new. More specifically, how soon is too soon?

Once again, when it comes to building a solid foundation with Mr. Next, a slow and steady progression trumps instant gratification every time. And here's why. When two people jump into bed together too quickly, they often mistake physical chemistry for emotional compatibility. (Been there, done him, right?) Hooked on the pheromone high of intoxicating makeout sessions, heavy petting, and steamy sex, two completely incompatible people can and will fall into the trap of thinking they're perfect for each other.

There's a reason I just used the term "trap." These individuals have just fallen prey to the sex trap. Convinced that the heat they feel for one another in the bedroom can transcend any other possible incompatibilities, they find themselves involved in an intimate relationship with someone they hardly know emotionally or intellectually.

As for that sex haze? It wears off. And then what happens? Lust leads to dust, as in this so-called love story bites the dust.

So what can you do to avoid such a fate? Take things slow in the beginning. I know, I know. I sound like your mother. But I'm not. I'm your relationship coach. And as a coach, I always advise my clients to take things slow in the beginning. Leave Mr. Next wanting more. Give him a taste of what you're offering, but ultimately hold out on jumping any guy's bones until you actually know each other.

So how long do you wait? Depends on the guy. Depends on you. But roughly speaking, seven to ten dates *and* a mutual agreement to be exclusive. Notice I said *and*, as in you can't have one without the other *and* still sleep with him.

Let me explain why. First, you shouldn't be sleeping with Mr. Next if you don't know who else he's sleeping with. Common sense and the Centers for Disease Control agree on this one—find out who he's swapping fluids with.

Second, you shouldn't sleep with someone just because you go out a few times. I mean, you can if you want but I don't recommend it. See, sex complicates dating. Translation: Sex complicates dating for women because regardless of what we say, we haven't quite figured out how to do it without getting emotionally attached. So why not postpone instant gratification for a few dates, at least until you both know if you want to keep seeing each other, *and* if you're comfortable with the idea of swapping fluids?

Facebook Friends Weigh In

When I asked the question *How soon is too soon to have sex with someone new?* on Facebook, here's what some of my fab friends said. . . .

"Wait at least five dates. Give the relationship time to grow before getting into bed with someone." —MAGGIE

"A lot of guys I meet online expect sex within the first few dates. I tell them 'No way.' If they're willing to wait, great. If not, I move on." —HEATHER

"There's no set timeline. Do what feels right for the relationship. Just don't rush into anything or feel pressured. Once you jump in, you can't take it back." —BARBARA

"Wait as long as possible. First date is definitely a no-no, go back to high school and draaaaaaaaawww the seduction out! Make them work for it. They prefer that anyways, even if they act like it's killing them." —TRISH

Here's the other thing. Until you're comfortable enough with a guy to broach the conversation of *Are you seeing other people?* and, more importantly, *Are we exclusive?* you shouldn't for one second believe that you're comfortable enough to get naked in front of him, let alone sleep with him.

Progress takes time and regardless of what your hormones are telling you, it's never time to jump into bed with some guy until you know that (A) he's not seeing anybody else, and (B) he wants to be exclusive with you. If you authentically accomplish that in less than seven to ten dates? Mazeltov. Boink yourselves silly. Until then, practice patience. And abstinence. If needed, invest in a fun new toy for yourself to stave off those hormonal surges.

When it comes to abstaining from physical intimacy early on in the dating process, I'm often asked, "How will a guy know if he wants to be exclusive with me if we haven't slept together yet? Isn't that part of his decision-making process?"

When it comes to *not* sleeping with a guy until you've had the exclusivity conversation, a lot of women buy into the belief system that no guy will commit to them without first having sex. And that may be true for some men. But quite honestly, do you want to date those guys? Do you really want your value in a casual dating relationship to be placed solely on your willingness to put out and how well you perform?

If so, good luck. But seriously, you're not a freakin' geisha or courtesan. You, my fabulous friend, are a living, breathing, thinking, valuable woman. You don't have to put out to prove it. And the right guy? The right Mr. Next will wait. As for the wrong guy? Good riddance.

Let me repeat that. You don't need to put out for every guy you date, nor do you have to put out with any one guy to get him to commit to you. Remember, one of your brand-spanking-new rules of dating is that you are a master multi-dater. And you can't exactly date and sleep with multiple people at the same time without earning a less than flattering reputation and putting your emotional and physical health at risk. So until you decide to stop playing the field and focus your fabulous energy and time on someone specific (and only if he's willing to do the same in return), sex does nothing more than complicate the game. And who wants to make dating *more* complicated?

Law of Attraction #3:
Unrequited Love Is *So* Not Sexy

So there's a cutie you're crushing on. He's sweet, smart, adorable, and . . . you don't know how he feels about you. Sure, he calls you, texts you, and makes time for you. But is he into you? Rather than waste any more of your precious time waiting around to find out (and in the process holding your heart hostage with wishful thinking), why not deal with the dilemma head-on? How? Talk to your crush about it. Yes, it's scary, but what's even scarier is the idea of you pining away silently for years, hung up on a hope that one day he'll come to his senses and declare his undying love for you.

Here's the deal with unrequited love. It's not real. It's actually just a fantasy playing over and over in your head that may feel exciting but is actually sabotaging your chances of relationship success. See, by being hung up on some guy who has no idea how you feel, you close your heart to other guys who may actually be into you.

So how exactly do you broach such a subject with your crush? You could do it as directly as I did. After years of secretly wishing, hoping, and crushing on my good guy friend, one day

I summoned the inner strength, dialed his digits, and flat out confessed, "So you know the other night when you dropped me off after the movie? I kind of wanted to kiss you."

His response: "Really? Wow. Yeah, I've thought about that. I don't know. Maybe we should try it sometime."

And then my crush hung up the phone, ran the other way, and avoided me like the plague for a month. But he did me a favor. By confessing to my crush and seeing him respond the way he did, it freed me up to meet other men. A month later, I met my husband. The rest, as they say, is history.

So maybe it will work out better with your unrequited crush. Or maybe not. But by being brave enough to deal with your feelings and stop waiting around and wishing, you pave the way for future relationship success—either with your crush or with someone unexpected and far more fabulous.

And in case you need further proof to determine whether or not your crush could be the real love deal, here are the top five ways to know if he's really into you:

- He's introduced you to his friends.
- He hangs out with you and your friends.
- He makes plans with you well in advance.
- He regularly drops hints about hooking up.
- He compliments you on your looks every time he sees you.

On the flip side, here are the top five signs your crush is *not* into you:

- He tells you about his dates with other women.
- He texts you all the time but never makes plans to get together.

- He forgets birthdays and other important occasions.
- He only makes last-minute plans with you.
- He consistently cancels plans at the last minute.

Coming out to your crush can be a nerve-racking experience, especially if things don't go as hoped. But again, by coming clean, you free yourself from the wishful-thinking trap you've been stuck in, and make room in your heart for the possibility of someone new. And at the end of the day, that's what's important—making yourself available for the right Mr. Nexts and absolutely unavailable for all those unsuspecting Mr. Wrongs.

Law of Attraction #4: Fall Head First, Not Heart First

So often in my coaching practice I see women falling for men who are not falling back. Yes, the guy likes the girl. Yes, he's having a good time. But is he falling in love? No. Is she? Yes. This is why it's essential to have the exclusivity conversation before jumping into a physical relationship.

Once you establish physical intimacy, it's much harder to emotionally disconnect. And you shouldn't jump into any new relationship without knowing if you're the only one jumping in. You are far too fabulous to fall for some guy if he's not falling for you in return. So the next time you're even tempted to fall for some guy, you owe it to yourself and your happily-ever-after future to check in with Mr. Next. See where his thoughts, energy, and intentions are. No, you don't have to flat out ask him if he's falling for you. But you should find out if he's seeing other people, if he's looking for an exclusive relationship, and if he sees a possible future with you.

Let me be clear. This is not first-date conversation material. But it's definitely fodder for a conversation somewhere between the fourth date and having breakfast in bed. Again, if you're not comfortable broaching the subject, then you shouldn't seriously consider sleeping with Mr. Next. Use that as an intimacy barometer.

1. When it comes to your dating life, which Law of Attraction have you been unconsciously breaking?

2. How will you implement all of the Laws of Attraction in your future dating life? Make an action plan and stick to it.

chapter 16

mr. next or mr. right?

At some point in your dating future, the time will come when you meet someone really special. Just hearing his voice will make you smile. Seeing him across a crowded room will quicken your pulse. And spending time together, no matter what you're doing, just feels effortlessly fabulous. When this happens, you'll wonder *Is this . . . could it be . . . is he The One*?

As exciting and nerve-racking as that will feel, it's important to keep a level head. After all, you've done a lot of work to heal your heart, become your most successful single self, and (hopefully) master the art of multi-dating. So before everything comes to a screeching halt and you decide to become a one-man woman, change your relationship status on Facebook, and cancel your online dating subscriptions, stop for a second. Take a step back. This is a big decision to make, and it shouldn't be made in haste. Before you two make that giant leap toward happily ever after, you need to first assess your situation. See what's really happening. Then approach Mr. Next to determine whether you're on the same page. The following guidelines will help you figure out if that special someone is Mr. Right or Mr. Right Now.

Love, Lust, or Just Plain Lost?

The first step in determining whether or not there's a future with Mr. Next is to figure out if what you've got is a case of love-in-training or just a hot-and-heavy helping of lust. Start by asking yourself the following five questions.

How Much Do You Really Know about Each Other's Lives?

Unsure if what you've got is love or lust? A great indicator is to assess how much you *really* know about Mr. Next's life. Sure, you may know what he does for a living and where he lives. You may even have each other's digits programmed into your cell phones. But have you met Mr. Next's friends, spent entire weekends together, been included in each other's daily lives? The best way to know if it's love or lust is take an honest look at how interconnected your life has become with Mr. Next's.

Are you still in date mode, seeing each other once or twice a week for a scheduled romantic activity (dinner, a movie, a concert, and so on) or do you devote whole evenings and weekends to hanging out, doing laundry, and running errands together? By being honest with yourself about the level at which you and Mr. Next are sharing and relating, you get a better idea of whether what you've got is the real deal or just sex appeal. The more entwined your lives have become, the more likely it is that you and Mr. Next have long-term relationship potential.

Is Your Physical Connection Stronger Than Your Emotional One?

Sometimes it's challenging to determine the difference between having the hots for someone and having what it takes to make a relationship work. A key deciding factor is to ask yourself what it is that you and Mr. Next actually have in common. Superficial commonalities like movies, food, partying, and passionate makeout sessions are most likely not enough to make a long-term relationship work. And that's okay. But do yourself and Mr. Next a favor by looking at your relationship realistically, starting right now.

Signs you may be involved in a predominantly lustful relationship with Mr. Next include:

- You jumped into a physical relationship within the first few dates (before you really knew each other).
- While your time between the sheets is magnetic, when you spend time together fully clothed, you run out of things to talk about, struggle to find common interests, and wonder what goes on inside his head most of the time.
- When you think about a future together, you have trouble envisioning what it looks like.

If the above signs seem familiar, it may be time to face the fact that your physical relationship is far more advanced than your emotional one. And honestly, there's not a whole lot you can do to remedy the situation. That's why it's important to take things slowly in the beginning of a new romantic encounter. If you dive into a physical relationship too soon, you sabotage your chances of ever building a strong emotional connection.

Already engaged in a hot and heavy romantic entanglement? Only you know for sure if this relationship can be saved. Honor your gut and acknowledge if and when it's time to cut your losses and move on. And don't force yourself to try and make something work simply because "we already slept together."

On the flip side, here are some surefire signs that your relationship is more than just a hearty case of lust:

- You and Mr. Next make time for one another on a regular basis.
- You and Mr. Next talk, text, and/or e-mail throughout the day.
- If you've already been intimate, you and Mr. Next regularly spend the entire night together (as well as most of the next morning).

Regardless of which scenario you find yourself involved in, it's important to be honest about where you and Mr. Next stand. Don't live in denial or try to pretend that what's happening is something other than what it really is. By being honest about the scope of your true feelings for Mr. Next (and vice versa), you avoid hurting each other in the long run. And at the end of the dating day, that's what's really important.

Do You Share Common Life Goals, Dreams, and Ambitions?

Before things get too hot and heavy between you and Mr. Next, you'll want to know what his long-term goals, dreams, and ambitions are. After all, you may not want to invest your time and energy in, let alone develop physical and emotional intimacy with, someone who doesn't share a similar future vision. Things you'll want to know before things get too hot and heavy include:

- What are each of your long-term relationship goals and do they match?
- Do you and Mr. Next share lifestyle priorities (career, home, marriage, and so on)?
- Do you and Mr. Next share similar ethics, morals, and values?
- Do you and Mr. Next share beliefs, goals, and timelines when it comes to wanting and starting a family?

While broaching these topics of conversation in the early stages of a relationship can feel intimidating, it's important to dive in and deal with them early on. Why? Because it forces both you *and* Mr. Next to communicate openly and honestly in hopes of cutting down on wasted time and hurt feelings. Plus, if you're already starting to engage in physical passion (or seriously considering taking the plunge), you'll want to make sure your emotional energy and long-term goals are equally compatible first.

Are the Feelings Mutual?

While you may feel that things are sailing along smoothly toward happily ever after, Mr. Next may have other ideas. Rather than find yourself headed toward *I do!* only to discover you've arrived all alone, it's essential to know where Mr. Next stands as soon as possible. This doesn't mean having a conversation about commitment on the first date, or offering an ultimatum about exclusivity on date #3. But as you find yourself getting more and more intimately involved, you need to know where you stand. And the only way to find out is to be brave enough to express your feelings and ask Mr. Next how he feels. If the feelings are not mutual—that is, if only one of you is interested in a casual physical relationship while the other one wants a future together—it's better to know before you've gotten too involved, both physically and emotionally.

Becoming intimately involved with someone new is exciting, exhilarating, and potentially excruciating if you're not on the same page. It's important to assess what's really going on early in the relationship, identify where you're both coming from, and determine whether or not you're compatible for long-term success. If and when you find yourself in a lust-only affair, it's up to you to act accordingly depending on your wants and needs. If you discover your passionate pursuit has future relationship potential, great! You may be well on your way to your new and improved happily ever after.

Red Light, Green Light?

So now that you've determined if what you and Mr. Next share could be love or will most likely never be more than just a strong case of lust, it's time to look for other important signs that he could in fact be Mr. Right. Start by asking yourself these oh-so-important questions.

Are You Listening to Your Gut?

Yes, he's cute. Funny? Of course! And he's even got a J-O-B. But what *else* is Mr. Next that you may be ignoring? The truth is, in our quest to redefine and re-experience our happily-ever-after future, we can sometimes turn a blind eye to who the guy we're dating really is. For example . . .

- Are you ignoring Mr. Next's general rude and crude behavior toward waiters, cab drivers, and bartenders because, well, he's so darn sweet to you?
- Are you looking the other way when his eye wanders to other pretty girls in the room because while he may be looking, Mr. Next isn't touching (except for you, of course)?
- Does his credit card get declined regularly, does he ask to borrow cash, and/or does it seem like Mr. Next's finances are in a constant state of crisis?
- Is he chronically late, constantly on his phone, or in any other way showing you disrespect on or between dates?

Here's the tough love truth about dating. Men don't necessarily mean to be jerks, but if they think they can get away with something, many will. If you stick around and put up with poor treatment including disrespect, constant criticism, or general emotional unavailability from Mr. Next, you silently condone his bad behavior. On the other hand, if you decide to walk away, hail a cab, and high tail it home when he misbehaves, Mr. Next will quickly learn what is and is *not* acceptable to you. If he changes his ways, he could be Mr. Right potential. If he doesn't, he's not worth the energy it takes to break up via text message.

So the next time your gut starts twitching when it comes to Mr. Next, it's up to you to act accordingly. Even if he *is* incredibly cute. Even if he just said he wants to take you away for the weekend. And most especially when he asks to borrow money for the umpteenth time and you know he'll never pay you back.

Have You Become a Seasoned Red-Flag Specialist?

Like those gut feelings you should always honor, savvy singles also come equipped with an effective alarm system that alerts you to red flags. Oftentimes the volume on this alarm system is turned down (or off!). As a result, you ignore red flags and find yourself getting involved with inappropriate partners because you're choosing to not pay attention. To successfully differentiate between Mr. Next and Mr. Right, it's essential to become a red-flag specialist. That means you *must* pay attention to red flags as Mr. Next reveals them to you.

Here are some examples of red-flag behaviors to watch out for.

- While Mr. Next claims he wants a long-term committed relationship, he's in his forties, has never been married, parties all weekend, and barely makes time for you (or any other woman) in his life.
- Even though he claims he's not seeing anyone else, you've noticed some flirty text messages on his cell phone from other women. When you ask about them, he denies knowing what you're talking about, and blames you for being an untrusting snoop.
- He says he loves his job, but he's constantly stressed, moody, and emotionally shut down after a day at the office.
- He says he'll call, e-mail, or text, but he doesn't—for weeks! Then, when he does, he expects you to drop everything and be there for him.

In a perfect world, you could take a man at his word. However, in the new millennium you have to be a bit of a super sleuth on the dating scene. That means paying attention to not only what a man says, but also how he says it, how his actions back up his words, and how he treats you, makes time for you, and interacts with the rest of the world. If his actions are out of alignment with his words, acknowledge those red flags and honor your instincts when they tell you to walk (or run!) away.

Do Either of You Play Unnecessary Games?

As a successful single, you owe it to yourself and Mr. Next not to play games (and vice versa). That means you call when you say you're going to call, do what you say you're going to do, and be honest when Mr. Next asks if you'd like to go out again. If you don't want to see him again, say so in a kind and considerate way. By being honest and letting him down easily, you avoid playing games. Expect the same in return. And if you get played, don't take your frustrations out on the next Mr. Next you date.

Top Five Signs He Could Be Mr. Right

Okay, so you've assessed your physical and emotional compatibility, become clear about how Mr. Right will and won't behave, and are getting a clearer understanding of whether Mr. Next qualifies to be a contender. Your next step is to see how Mr. Next's behavior stacks up to five essential qualities Mr. Right possesses. Read on for details.

Quality #1: He Listens to You

The best way to know if Mr. Next is interested in (and worthy of) being a candidate for Mr. Right? He *listens* to you.

You'll know he's listening when he shows genuine concern, consistently remembers things you've told him (your birthday, favorite food, best friend's name, and so on), and offers emotional support in honest and thoughtful ways. If your current Mr. Next exhibits the signs of a thoughtful listener, he's still in the running to becoming Mr. Right.

Quality #2: You Share an Effortless Ease

We've all been in those relationships that take W-O-R-K (and suck the life force out of us in the process). When a relationship works on its own, it feels effortless, easy, and fluid. You don't have to force anything, forgive anything, or turn a blind eye to red flags or gut-twisters. Instead, you and Mr. Next communicate and collaborate with comfort, compatibility, and undeniable chemistry. If and when you experience this kind of interaction with Mr. Next, you may be on to something really special.

Quality #3: You Don't Have to Compromise Who You Are

So often, women feel the need to sacrifice some part of themselves to make a relationship work. In the right relationship, there's no need. You don't have to hide, tone down, or apologize for any aspect of your fabulous life. With the right partner, you're not only able to be yourself, but you're better able to be the best version of your most authentic self, no compromises needed.

Quality #4: You Trust Him

A relationship without trust is doomed from the start. But a relationship with abundant trust? A fabulous foundation for real and lasting love. Built over time, trust is based on the simple belief system that Mr. Next has your best interests at heart and will never intentionally hurt you (and vice versa). If and when you discover that Mr. Next is 100 percent trustworthy, you'll have no trouble giving your heart to him. In return, he'll most likely give you his heart and pave the way for a lasting, loving relationship to unfold.

Quality #5: He Enriches Your Life

In the wrong relationship, your partner tears you down, bums you out, and in general drains your energy. In the right relationship, Mr. Next enriches your life, inspires you to be your best self, and in general brings a sense of peace and possibility to you. You'll know Mr. Next is enriching your life if and when he encourages and supports you professionally, personally, and spiritually. And when he does, he may just be Mr. Right!

Mr. Next, Meet Mr. Right

And finally, once you've assessed whether it's lust or potentially love, scanned your budding romance with Mr. Next for red flags and gut-twisters, and sized him up against the top five qualities Mr. Right possesses, it's time to make your final decision. Is Mr. Next worthy of the title of Mr. Right?

If all signs point to *Woohoo!*, then congratulations! You have done your homework, chosen wisely, and are now well positioned for success. (If not, pick yourself up, dust yourself off, and get back into the dating pool.) Of course, there's one final hurdle you and Mr. Next must conquer. It's time to ask the all-important question. . . .

"Where do you see this going?"

Admittedly, this is one of the scariest questions you may ever ask Mr. Next. Then again, if you're at the stage where you're considering giving your heart to him, you've got to be brave and bold and go for it. Unsure how and when to pop the question? Here are some valuable dos and don'ts:

Don't: Bring it up when you know you're short on time.

Do: Bring it up casually, when the two of you are relaxed.

Don't: Approach the conversation with anger, tears, or negativity.

Do: Come from a place of kindness, compassion, and honesty.

Don't: Make demands, use emotional blackmail, or issue ultimatums.

Do: Love yourself enough to ask with confidence.

Don't: Try to talk him out of how he feels.

Do: Respect yourself enough to handle his response, whatever it is, with dignity.

By following these guidelines, the exclusivity conversation will be no big deal. If you and Mr. Next are on the same page, and both want to move the relationship forward, fantastic! You have successfully found Mr. Right. (If not, it's better to know now than to wait until you're more emotionally and physically connected.)

So where do you and Mr. Right go from here? Step by step into your fabulous happily-ever-after future. Remember that it won't always be smooth sailing, but by respecting each other, communicating as honestly and openly as you can, and coming from a place of kindness and compassion, you are well on your way to a blissful life together.

1. Ready to put your budding relationship to the love or lust test? Review the five questions that determine whether it's love or lust. Where do you and Mr. Next stand?

2. Are there red flags or gut-twisters in your budding relationship that you're ignoring? If so, be honest and identify them before you continue any further down the road with Mr. Next.

3. Put Mr. Next to the test, identifying how many of Mr. Right's five qualities he possesses.

Results

So . . . what are the results? Share them with me at IfHesNot TheOneWhoIs.com!

conclusion

Can you believe you've reached the end of this book? I feel like our journey together is just beginning—and that's because it is. First, I want to congratulate you for being such a rock star and reading all the way to the end. I know there were most likely times when you wanted to close the book and move on to something that involved less work. But you didn't. And I appreciate that.

Whether you know it or not, walking away from the pain of your past and into a more hopeful future is one of the most rewarding gifts you'll ever give yourself. It shouldn't end when you close this book. This really is just the beginning of a whole new happily-ever-after journey for you. And I'd like to be your guide. I invite you to visit IfHesNottheOneWhoIs.com. There you'll find some valuable resources and FREE bonuses that I know you'll love. And feel free to drop me a line to let me know how your journey's going, you can do that, too. The choice is yours. Know that I'm always here for you, and that your brilliant future is ready and waiting for you to discover.

To your success!

XOXO,

Lisa

about the author

Lisa Steadman is an internationally known author, speaker, and success coach dedicated to helping women move away from the pain of the past and into their brilliant futures. She regularly contributes to the media, including appearances on *The Today Show*, *The Tyra Banks Show*, Playboy Radio, and New Zealand's *Good Morning*. Lisa lives in Southern California with her husband. She can be found at LisaSteadman.com.